T0329059

# POETICS OF RAGE

### (A Reading of Remi Raji's Poetry)

# Other Books by Sule E. Egya

## Fiction
*Dream and Shame*
*Impotent Heavens*

## Poetry
*What the Sea Told Me*
*Naked Sun*
*Knifing Tongues*

## Non-Fiction
*In Their Voices and Visions: Conversations with
New Nigerian Writers Vol. I*

# POETICS OF RAGE
### (A Reading of Remi Raji's Poetry)

**Sule E. Egya**

KRAFT BOOKS LIMITED

*Published by*

**Kraft Books Limited**
6A Polytechnic Road, Sango, Ibadan
Box 22084, University of Ibadan Post Office
Ibadan, Oyo State, Nigeria
℗ 0803 348 2474, 0805 129 1191
E-mail: kraftbooks@yahoo.com

First published 2011

ISBN 978-978-918-015-8

= KRAFTGRIOTS =
(A literary imprint of Kraft Books Limited)

First printing, November 2011

# Dedication

To the fond memory of late Dr. Pius Olusegun Dada, my teacher and friend.

# Acknowledgements

Out of this research a number of academic papers have been published. "The Nationalist Imagination in Remi Raji's *Lovesong for My Wasteland*" appeared in *Research in African Literatures*, volume 38, number 4. "Transnational Imagination: Remi Raji's Poetic Travelogue" appeared in *Nasarawa Journal of Humanity* volume 2, number 2. "A Critique of the Images of the Oppressor in Remi Raji's Poetry" appeared in *Ibadan Journal of English Studies*, number 2. "The Poet on Military Misrule: A Study of Remi Raji's *Webs of Remembrance*" appeared in *Benue Valley Journal of Humanities*, volume 1, number 6. "'Your Breath into My Breath': an Exploration into Remi Raji's Love Poems in *A Harvest of Laughters*" (co-authored with Ismail Garba Bala) appeared in *Currents in African Literature and the English Language: Journal of ICALEL*, volume 5.

This work has benefitted immensely from the guidance and suggestions of Prof. Sophia Ogwude, Prof. Kanchana Ugbabe and Dr. Gboyega Kolawole. I am grateful to them for putting me in the right direction.

I have also, in the course of this work, interacted with other scholars such as Amanze Akpuda, Ismail Bala Garba, Dr GMT Emezue, Dr Aderemi Raji-Oyelade, Dr KBC Ashipu, Dr Ferdinand Asoo, Dr. Melita Aleksa, Elizabeth Onogwu and Jacob Olotu. Their ideas have strengthened this work a great deal.

To quite a number of others whose names do not appear here, I say thank you.

# Preface

One evening in 2003, during the convention of Association of Nigerian Authors in Makurdi, Benue State, I was chatting with one of my teachers when the poet Remi Raji interrupted us and gave her a collection of his poetry. Jokingly, I demanded for mine. After a brief acquaintance, he dipped his hand into his bag, brought out a copy of *Webs of Remembrance* and autographed it for me. That night it was my companion. Beyond that, it triggered my interest in not only Remi Raji's poetry but also the poetry of his generation. Subsequently, I have centred my scholarly energies on understanding and explicating the challenges and struggles, the commitment and vision, of this poetry.

This book is therefore one of my modest attempts to appreciate, interpret and canonise the new poetry in Nigeria that has emerged, historically, contextually, from the decades of militarisation and the ongoing bastardisation of democratic norms in Africa. In this scholarly exercise, I have young researchers in mind and that informs my resolve to express myself in a language as lucid as possible, though far from being jargon-free. Part of the reasons undergraduate and graduate students shy away from exploring new writing in Africa today is because scholars, and this is appalling, have forged little or no inroad into new writing; they have failed to introduce new writing in elaborately canonical templates. Thus, the complaint of young researchers that there are "no materials" on new writing is, aside from the endemic laziness in the system, germane. My major objective here is to invite young researchers and scholars to a debate on not only Remi Raji's poetry but the poetry of his generation. The socio-political and historical context of Remi Raji's poetry is one that is shared by almost all poets of his time. Even in matters of form and structure there is a great deal of things common to the poets of this era as I intend to show in my other endeavours.

Given the thematic focus of the book, I have arranged my treatments of Remi Raji's volumes not according to their years of production as some readers might expect but according to their feasibility to my frame of discourse. Hence, the chapter on *Gather My Blood Rivers of Song*, Remi Raji's latest volume as at the time this book was finished, comes before the one on *Shuttlesongs: America – A Poetic Guided Tour*, his third volume. Also for the same reason, some of Remi Raji's poems are not treated in this book. That I focus my discourse on Remi Raji's political poetry does not mean that he does not write poems about other spheres of life. But, as I hope to show, there is something *inherently* political even in his private poems. And this is characteristic of his restless, angry generation.

**Sule E. Egya**
Keffi.

For a long time I took my pen for a sword.

–*Jean-Paul Sartre*

# Contents

# CHAPTER

# 1

## Introduction: Location of Remi Raji's Political Poetics

This study explores the nationalist imagination, artistic philosophy and the overtly political dimension of Remi Raji's poetry. It is an attempt to construct a sustained critical discourse on Raji's ongoing body of works. Raji is one of the major poetic voices on the Nigerian literary scene today. With the publication of his first collection, *A Harvest of Laughters*, in 1997 Raji has continued to strengthen his craft and vision through subsequent volumes: *Webs of Remembrance* (2000), *Shuttlesongs: America – a Poetic Guided Tour* (2003), *Lovesong for My Wasteland* (2005); and *Gather My Blood Rivers of Song* (2009). Evidently he has attained poetic maturity and, given the frequency of his output, is set to realise a fulfilled poetic career. His maturation thus far through these five volumes deserves a major critical assessment, and a possible prediction for the direction of his artistic vision.

Like his contemporaries, even more like his precursors in African poetry in European languages, Raji devises an idiom, realises an aesthetic, utterly sensitive to the plight of the society, largely responsive to the failure of leadership in his country. His poetry does not shy away from this fact, nor veil them in any *avant-garde* formalism. In fact, his poetry easily, readily, betrays that socialist outrage that tends to dwarf techniques in African poetry. The poem is, first, about rescuing the society, before it is about rhythm and rhyme. Inaugurating his political theme with the metaphor of laughter in his first collection, he pursues it with the metaphor of love in his fourth, and further consolidates it with the metaphor of blood in the fifth. In these poetic strategies,

Raji is basically concerned with the fate of his nation, Nigeria, having passed through a terrible military era and emerged still into an inconsequential, trivialised democracy. While his earlier volumes, charged with optimism, concern themselves with the military oppression of the past decades, his latest collection centres on the infantile, corrupted democracy, and the betrayal of the people's hope, especially those who made (even the ultimate) sacrifices to ensure the dethronement of military oppression in Nigeria.

It is in this light that we mainly tag Raji's poetry political here. We may take political poetry as that variety of poetry that depicts and declaims the failure of leadership; that captures the helpless masses suppressed and oppressed by the establishment; that, whether moulded in optimism or pessimism, engages the society, the people, in charting a positive discourse of nation formation. This kind of poetry, belonging to the domain of protest literature, shouts, barks, screams, cries, curses, swears and prays in dire resignation, with the intent, most often, to awaken the consciousness of its audience, and to challenge, even if ineffectually, the regime of oppression silencing the society. It is also a poetry that establishes a two-dimensional dialogue: one, between the poet and the people for whom the poet claims to undertake a selfless duty; and, two, between the poet and the oppressor-figure who the poet relentlessly attacks with what one might see as *violent* metaphors. Ingrained in, but not limited to, post-colonial literatures, political poetry is a manifestation of committed writing that comes with the realisation of the poet that his poetic vision must transcend the abstraction of artistic self-glorification. In transcending poetic subjectivity, the political poet objectifies his voice through what Remi Raji himself calls "the aesthetics of rage" (3). Expounding committed writing in the afterword to his recent volume of poetry, *The Dreamer, His Vision*, Gabriel Okara submits that "[the] poet must exist to exercise the powers of the Word to realise his visions and an existing society on which he focuses his visions" (78). First, the poet has "powers" from his manipulation, refiguration, of words, his immersion in imagery; second, such powers, translating into vision, an emphatic conceptualisation of nationhood, must be focused on the well being of a people. The political poet considers himself organically linked to his nation, eager to speak with a fearless voice, to pursue interrogations, to seek answers and to evaluate societal orthodoxies on behalf of the ordinary people. The American poet Robert Bly, in an essay on political poetry, rather sees the enterprise of the political poet as engagement with the "psyche" of the nation. He posits that "the life of the nation can be imagined...as a psyche larger than the psyche of anyone living, a larger sphere, floating above everyone. In order for the poet to write a true political poem, he has to be able to have such a grasp of his own concerns that he can leave them for a while, and then leap up into this other psyche" (100). Bly juxtaposes a national psyche with an individual psyche, a design that can better capture the poetic engagements of the early Nigerian poets namely Christopher Okigbo, Wole Soyinka, J. P. Clark and others. But we may find Bly's demarcation between individual psyche and national psyche, requiring the poet to leap from one to the other, as Okigbo is said to have leapt from his psyche to his nation's (see, for example, *Towards the Decolonization of African Literature*), inadequate in the situation of Raji's generation of poets. As I intend to show in this study, there is really no demarcation between the concern of the individual and that of the nation, at least since the inception, and the assertive presence, of what has come to be known as the alter-native tradition (Aiyejina112-128), because the individual is inextricably, inseparably tied to the nation; the poet considers his voice as originating from the society, belonging to the society, and dedicated to the wellbeing of the society.

Contemporary Nigerian poetry as used in this work, or as a context for the characterisation of Raji's poetry, refers to the poetry of Raji's contemporaries. Some of them are at the stage Raji is, in the heyday of their maturation, almost reaching the peak of their writing careers. Some of them are stagnant after their debuts, weighed down by lack of publishing prospect, perilous socio-political condition, and the often unexpected discomfort of exile and migration. A historical finger would pin the emergence of this generation of writers, now widely known as the third generation of modern writers in Nigerian literary canon, to 1988.[1] This is the year the critic and scholar Harry Garuba published a definitive anthology of one hundred new Nigerian poets entitled *Voices from the Fringe*. It is this seminal volume that ushers this generation into the Nigerian literary scene. Some of the *serious* poets of this period who, like Raji, have made valid contributions to the artistic mould of their era are Olu Oguibe, Uche Nduka, Chiedu Ezeanah, Ogaga Ifowodo, Toyin Adewale, Abubakar Othman, and Maik Nwosu. An exploration of the poetry of this generation shows that the poets, like their predecessors (those who wrote before them and are still writing along with them), subscribe to the African philosophy of social commitment in art. Most of the poetry of this era is, like the poetry of the alter-native tradition, preoccupied with political concerns because of the poets' consciousness to take a stand against the overwhelming socio-political inadequacies of his society. Early in African literature, Chinua Achebe has pointed out that "an African creative writer who tries to avoid the big social and political issues of contemporary Africa will end up being completely irrelevant" (*Morning Yet on Creation Day, 78*). Nigerian writers, in spite of their disparate ideological persuasions, have had faith in this statement and seen their writing as a means to respond to critical social issues and make decisive statements. The new poets have used their creative imagination to capture the despondencies caused by military dictatorships in Nigeria from the 1980s to the 1990s. The dictatorships of General Ibrahim Badamasi Babangida and late General Sani Abacha, spanning the aforementioned decades, brought untold hardship to Nigerians.[2] Up till today, Nigeria is yet to recover from the dispossession, suppression and oppression that came with those regimes. There have been personal accounts and social commentaries, along with a steady growth of literary explorations, on the intensity of the oppression of those decades, such as Kunle Ajibade's *Jailed for Life*, Chris Anyawu's *The Days of Terrors*, and Karl Maier's *This House Has Fallen*. The poets, as well as the writers of other genres, attempt to chronicle those years and expose the cruelty of those dictators. Apart from historicising the years of plundering, they also dwell philosophically on the current psychic collapse in the land, which is a natural consequence of the military despotism. Thus, "[this] generation of Nigerian writers has had to deal with disillusionment in every aspect of the Nigerian state, especially political" (Azuah 24).

For these poets then writing becomes a kind of cultural struggle that goes parallel with other kinds of cultural struggle such as protest music, guerrilla journalism and coordinated demonstrations all aimed at unseating the despotism of the 1990s in Nigeria. In most cases, the poets are also activists, giving the impression that sometimes craft is insufficient in the struggles against military dictatorships. Raji's poetry clearly captures the temperament of this age, offers an insight into the exerting contradictions in the nation under the military era, and dramatises the irrepressible voices of the diverse forces that constituted themselves to face the sheer antics and bare cruelty of the despotic rulers.

### Remi Raji: The Poet and His Vision
Born in Ibadan in 1961, Raji attended his primary school, Nurul Islamiyya Primary School, in southeast Ibadan. He finished in 1973 and proceeded to a secondary school, Holy Trinity Grammar School, the same year. After taking his Higher School Certificate at Olivet Baptist High School, Oyo, in 1979, he went to University of Ibadan to study English. He took his first degree in 1984, took his second degree in 1986 and got his PhD in 1992, all at Ibadan. After having a stint elsewhere as a teacher, he has been teaching in the Department of English, University of Ibadan. Raji's poetry

has won both local and international awards: *A Harvest of Laughters* was a joint winner of the Association of Nigerian Authors / Cadbury Poetry Prize in 1997; had a honourable mention in the Okigbo National Poetry Prize in the same year; and won Association of West African Young Writers' VOCA Award for the Best First Published Book of the Year in 1997. A well-travelled writer and scholar, Raji has read his poems to local audiences and audiences in Africa, the United States, and Europe.

Raji's poetry, transcending any private agenda, carries a vision anchored in a past plundered and wasted, in a present burdened with frustration and anguish and in a future envisaged with surpassing optimism. His poetry is full of a cry of hope for a people. It is the kind of poetry that seeks to reach out to the masses, eager to, in M. S. C. Okolo's words, "prompt people to seek justice for and to criticise their political situation" (1). Raji is consistent in his poetic vision and has always seen himself as a poet with a "nationalist imagination" (*Webs of Remembrance*, 9). He follows the steps of writers in Africa who, in spite of the obvious, choose to *pronounce* loudly an organic connection between their writing and their society. Here is how Raji explains his indebtedness to his nation as a poet:

> There are levels of nationalism. I mean there are false nationalisms and there are critical nationalisms. The idea was to look back at my country and to do a critique of society because most people, poets, sometimes, try to run away from the possibilities of connecting poetry and pure nationalism. Even though I wrote these poems all at different times, I suddenly realized that most of the things I was talking about had to do with the country, all forms of oppressions, different kinds of silences. One major thing that connects all of them is that nationalist imagination. (*Sou'wester*, 10)

Most of Raji's collected poems are deeply political, demonstrating the inexhaustible energies of a patriotic poet ready, again in his own words,

> to engage in intimate dialogues and interrogation of years
> and decades of despondency, to confront the outrage of
> tyranny, to plant hope where none is imagined, to explode
> the myth of silence and give voice to the speechless, to
> pluck laughter from the howling winds ... and, above all,
> to be the active child of Optimism in the midst of dire
> Pessimism. ("The Aesthetics of Rage" 3)

This is certainly a huge agenda for a poet. It is this duty that African writers, committed to a nationalist vision, have pursued since the beginning of African literature, which Charles Nnolim, in his assessment of it, sees as "lachrymal" ("African Literature in the 21st Century", 1) because of the history of slavery and colonialism behind it.

Raji's period of gestation and maturation as a poet – a period, from the 1980s, that covers what has now come to be known as the third generation of Anglophone Nigerian writers – is a period from which a poet, a writer, cannot ignore drawing his thematic concerns. Those were the years of hardship, oppression and plunder in Nigeria perpetrated by cruel military dictators. The terrible memories of those years have continued to fertilise creative writings. They form the springboard for the harvest of political poetry in Nigeria today. As an active player in this domain, Raji writes poetry that portrays "the havoc of yesterday's flood" (*Webs of Remembrance*, 9) and attempts to lift his audience out of this havoc by sowing a seed of optimism in them through a constant motif seen in his philosophical elevation of laughter. He sees himself as a namesake of laughter. It is in this laughter that the seed of hope for the bright future is encapsulated. He says he has "never looked back at the dark side of life. [He looks] forward to the brighter moments. So the journey is certainly from the darkness to light" (*Sou'wester*, 12).

But Raji has been in a critical dialogue with the evaluators of his poetry. His poetry is fine and worth giving an ear, they do not doubt that. They, however, see him as *imitating* Niyi Osundare, probably the most important poet in Nigeria today who did mentor Raji at some time in his formative period. Raji does not claim that he is absolutely free of any influence from Osundare, after all Osundare did not only teach him Creative Writing, Osundare's poetry has been quite inspirational to most, if not all, younger poets writing in Nigeria today. During the 6th Lagos Book and Art Festival, in an open discussion in which the issue of Osundare's heavy influence on him was raised, Raji responded to the issue thus:

> In those days, Niyi Osundare used to tell me that I wrote too much like Wole Soyinka.... He and Okpewho kept nudging me to evolve my own writing. Looking back now, I believe these older writers and myself write from the same cultural pool. ("Daily Independent", E8)

Raji throws up an important issue here: the cultural pool contextualising writing in Nigeria. This pool is both thematic and stylistic. Thematically Raji, like his predecessors, confronts the leadership question; stylistically Raji, like his predecessors, roots his art in Yoruba traditional lore. In this broadly elastic pool there are other poets, also of Yoruba origin, that can be located; it is a pool that eventually mutates into what T. S. Eliot calls a literary tradition.

It is however pertinent to point out that similarities abound between Osundare's poetry and Raji's poetry. These similarities, parts of a larger texture of a literary tradition, should not be taken in a negative sense. It is perhaps better to begin by showing that similarities, if contextually understood, also abound between other older poets' poetry and Raji's poetry. Raji's nurturing of poetic vision, through a consistency of running imagery, is similar to Christopher Okigbo's. We can see Raji's poetry as one long poem because of the organic links of his continuous images as Darthone has made us see in Okigbo's poetry in his essay, "A Study of Two Poems: Okigbo Understood."[3] We can see the passion Dennis Brutus has for his land phenomenalised in a love affair in Raji's poetry. Even the rage with which Raji hurls images at the failed leaders in his country is similar to the rage with which

Brutus attacks the Apartheid system. And yet we see Aime Cessaire in Raji in his deployment and tidying up of images; one image dissolves into another almost seamlessly. More over, we can see the Diopian optimism for Africa (See, for instance, Ngara 27-32) in Raji's glowing hope for Nigeria which reverberates through his poetry. The foregoing shows that a poet, like every other artist, is in a web of artistic production in which voices mingle and intertextually dialogue with one another. While a poet may choose to consciously include himself (as Raji does) or exclude himself in a literary tradition or in a web of artistic production, it is also, in my view, a valid point to say that no writer at any point is free of literary inspirations and influences.

The major similarity between Osundare's poetry and Raji's poetry is that they are both imbued with the spirit of song and the poets themselves sometimes wrongly call them songs. For Osundare and Raji, who write from the same Yoruba cultural roots where song is a natural springboard for artistry (in fact, Raji started his artistic career as a Fuji singer), every poetic thought has to come in songful rhythms.[4] They both use material from Yoruba folk wisdom, as in their idiomatisation of the Yoruba concept of laughter clearly put in their intertextually related titles: *Waiting Laughters* and *A Harvest of Laughters*. Another similarity is that Osundare and Raji, as well as most writers from Nigeria, share the same theoretical view namely literature is an ideological weapon used for the struggle for survival, for the emancipation of the land from its suffocating socio-political problems. The poetry of this philosophy, which most Nigerian poets write, must embody social messages. Their poetry "speaks directly into the topical debates of modern Nigeria" (Brown104-105). The diction of such poetry goes soft and audience-patronising. And, as Donatus Nwoga points out, the poet fulfils his "wish to communicate with the masses" (48). Theme is therefore a meeting point for their poetry. But there are philosophical and even stylistic differences between the poetry of Osundare and that of Raji. Osundare's social vision is discursive and almost versatile; he does not, like Raji, create images that make the body of his poetry run through as a single poem. Raji's poetry seems to be straitjacketed into the nationalist imagination. Even when Raji writes love poems, we discern the nationalist imagination in them. While Osundare's satirical poems may spur laughter, Raji's satirical poems hardly do so. Raji, unpretentious with his images, has obvious rage that does not easily give way to humour. The seriousness of Osundare's poetry is often encapsulated in what Stewart Brown calls "its lightness of touch" (105). Osundare's "Sule chase", for example, succeeds as a satire because of its humour. While Raji comes out as an angry poet, quite combatant in his stand against the bad leaders, Osundare, with his almost always sprung rhythm (see, for instance, Fioupou 179-195), comes out as an angry but chuckling poet, with a theatrical, carnivalesque sense of protest. Osundare's poetry is generously flowered with Yoruba words and idioms, easily betraying their traditional influences. Raji's poems written in English (he also writes poems in Yoruba) do not easily contain Yoruba words. Raji's poetry is not as proverb-packed as Osundare's poetry. What this means is that Raji's poetry, more than Osundare's, maintains a distance (not a disconnection) between itself and the Yoruba culture. Raji, unlike Osundare, is not given to writing long poems. In Raji's fourth volume of poetry, Lovesong for my Wasteland, a single poem in forty-five verses, we can still read the verses as short individual poems, unlike Osundare's Waiting Laughters (1990) and Midlife (1993). Both poets are eloquent, but while Osundare's eloquence is more felt in his skilful use of repetition and other musical devices, Raji's eloquence is more felt in the brevity of his poetic sparks.

Raji has become a notable poetic voice, profoundly rooted in Nigerian literary tradition, but increasingly internationalising his voice and seeking global audience. His vision has been steady; his craft has gone through stages of refinement and renewal. To establish the foregoing is the major concern of this study.

## The Form and Style of Raji's Poetry

The poet's major preoccupation is with the language, the form and the structure of his poem, his art. It is his major preoccupation because it distinguishes him from a journalist, an essayist or even a fiction writer. The primacy of language in poetry has never been in doubt, but its institution has varied from place to place, tradition to tradition. Phil Roberts, in his book, *How Poetry Works*, points out that "[w]hat the poem articulates is, in the end, itself" (62). Poetry, then, has the tendency not to condescend, or patronise, or apologise; it is often the essence of *arrogant* craft. The reader comes to it with his senses alert, especially the auditory sense. A poem is like a piece of music, emphasising on what is *heard*, not what is *known*, following what Suzanne Langer calls "the morphology of feeling" (quoted in Roberts 62). If the poet, well schooled in his craft, deploys linguistic items, the referentiality of the items, which has nothing to do with "the morphology of feeling", is, strictly speaking, secondary to the manner in which he deploys the items. When, for instance, Raji writes, "To love is to gather my blood into a river of songs", he invites us primarily to a dialogue, not only with the referentiality of the lexical items: love, gather, blood, river, songs; but, more importantly, to behold the beauty of collocating the items in a way that is outside the confines of everyday speech. A poet worth his craft is constantly struggling to dazzle us, to engage us, to stretch our sensibility, with such language play, often unmindful of meanings, knowing fully that it is by refiguring the language, taking advantage of its elasticity, that he can hold his audience. Poets like Raji who are politically conscious are committed to language in a way that the language is *made* to carry out extra function other than the aesthetic display of the linguistic items. Their idioms, in terms of content and form, are conditioned by the transformative powers of the words since the words are deliberately deployed to *alter* situations. For such poets, then, their preoccupation with language is, first, to have a proper sense of artistry with words and, second, to have the skills to engage the words in extra-artistic commitment. It is in this sense the French writer and philosopher Jean-Paul Sartre considers language, the language of the literary artist, as a form of armament, a kind of lethal substance with which writers can (should) hit at the heart of the establishment.[5]

It is needless to say that, like most African poets, Raji writes in blank verse. But as Dasylva and Jegede have pointed out in their *Studies in Poetry*, "[f]ree verse does not suggest metric liberty, it simply means that the control of the verse is informed by the poet's own emotion or stream of consciousness and not by an external order or rule" (21). Raji's poems do not exhibit any evidences of external prescription in the form of metrical feats or rhyming schemes, but the internal rhythms are discernible by any keen reader of poetry. In the first poem in *A Harvest*, we notice the internal rhythm; a good ear can hear the falling and rising, and the assonated syllables when these lines are read aloud:

> No, not for me the twilight tales
> of sick knights
> not for me, the wilting metaphors
> of pain-wrights. (4-7)

Or the ascending rhythm in the following lines taken from "The city: in three tongues" (*Gather My Blood*):

> Do not
> Do not go
> Do not go to that city
> Where melodies are made
> With the skulls of men. (2-7)

This shows that Raji is conscious of the arrangement of his words in expressing his thoughts. This rhythm, when deployed skilfully as Raji does in some cases, results in musicality although this cannot happen without the use of other sound effects.

As is demonstrated in his corpus, Raji's poems are mostly lyrical, short, either written in stanzas or in run-on lines. They sometimes come through as songs because of the beats and controlled rhythms. A great deal of lyricism is achieved in Raji's third and fourth collections of poems, which are, as their titles suggest, seen as songs by the poet: *Shuttlesongs: America – a Poetic Guided Tour* and *Lovesong for My Wasteland*. The rhythms and beats are not just heightened, the diction of these collections become softer, fitting into what we may call the 'linguisticality' of song.[6] Quite musical is this example from *Shuttlesongs: America*,

And that Sunday summer noon
When Katherine suddenly
became a mermaid
Ridin' and rollin' down down the river
Showing us how not to drown
Ridin' and rollin' down down the river
How not to become new legends
In Kalamazoo's native tales...
If the river is not too deep
It is long in breath and brown with age.
Tom was with me, Tom was with her
Two canoes... (18)

The grammatical contractions, the repetitions, the parallelisms, the alliterations, assonances and consonances, and the limpidity of the imagery all move the poem towards the rhythms and beats of a song. Conscious that he is writing lyrical poems that best sound as songs, Raji, in his author's note to *Shuttlesongs: America*, says that "I have seen historic places therefore I memorize these into movement of songs..." (vii). The transformation of lyrical poems into songs is not peculiar to Raji's poetry alone. In fact, it has increasingly become a trend for Nigerian poets, since the post-war generation, to see poems as songs. The rhythms and diction of poetry thus become patterned in the manner of songs. In his introduction to Emman Usman Shehu's collection *Open Sesame*, Harry Garuba confirms this when he writes,

The poetic style favours the simple rhyme, or even the cliché that matches the movement that clinches the pattern of the dance steps. This is because the poem is not conceived as just words on paper ... the words strive to imitate the musicality of the song-lyric and the rhythm of dance-movement. (*xi*)

This tendency to conceive of poems as songs by the poets themselves may not, as the low standard of artistry in contemporary poetry in Nigeria indicates, be of any positive effects on the literary scene because it implies (sometimes erroneously) that the language of poetry has become weak.

In each volume of his poetry, Raji seems to have what we may call a programmatic trope, that is, a personal, signifying trope to undergird his poetic vision. In *A Harvest*, for instance, the developed or master trope is laughter; in *Lovesong*, it is love; and in *Gather My Blood*, the trope, though not elaborated as in others (and this speaks volume about the eclecticism of the volume), is blood. He presents these tropes or idioms as mediums through which he sustains his dialogue with the people on behalf of whom he writes. These two lines from "Harvest I-VI" (*A Harvest*) underscore Raji's vision in the collection: "grim-faced brother, Laughter can heal / if only you know..." (22-23).

Raji writes in Standard English and not in Pidgin Nigerian English, like some of his contemporaries, notably, Ezenwa-Ohaeto. In spite of the elliptical nature of the English phraseology in poetry, Raji endeavours to construct phrases that are not far-fetched. In his early poetry, in which he deploys the rich resources of language in constructing intense imagery, a reader does not have to worry about interpreting the surface meaning of the lines.[7] There is nothing lexically and semantically complex about such lines as "the blighted clouds of a locust rain" (taken from "I rise now" in *A Harvest*); "it was the dimple breath of dawn / growing deep on my palms like a new love" (taken from "Black laughter" in *A Harvest*); "and i smell the odour in the air / which betrays the anus of the tribe / dressed but naked like prostitutes..." (taken from "Bound to Remember" in *Webs of Remembrance*); "From the seashore and sandsheets of dreams / your eyes show me centuries of journeys" (taken from "Interlude: dance" in *Webs of Remembrance*); and "will you bury the anger in the coffin of laughter?" (taken from "Questions and Prayers" in *Gather My Blood*). It is however pertinent to point out that each line above evokes an image and reading them without recourse to the deeper meanings they contain will amount to not understanding them at all. Raji, in evolving a style leaning on poetical eloquence, prefers to, in Ezenwa-Ohaeto's words, 'eliminate lexical impediments, unclog poetic syntax" (*Contemporary Nigerian Poetry*, 11) so that the lines, beyond acquiring a phonic essence, engage the sensibility of the reader in a manner that is tasking but pleasant. To this extent, Raji's language and style cannot be said to be complex nor simple though this researcher has had to take him to task on the nature of imagery in *Shuttlesongs: America* (see *In Their Voices and Visions*, 74-91). It is in this light that the charge of writing in watery literary language levelled against most political poets in Nigerian literature should not be brought against Raji. In his book, *Understanding African Poetry*, Ken Godwin calls attention to the declining quality of literary language, especially in politically engaged poetry:

> For a poet committed to poetry as a political instrument, literary quality may seem of little importance: an irrelevance or even a subversive hindrance. It is not surprising, then, that the politicisation of African poetry in English has been accompanied by a decline in literary quality. (xiii)

Godwin's assertion here is similar to an on-going debate on the quality of literary language not only in Nigerian poetry, but also in poetry written elsewhere in the world. A number of critics and writers such as Tanure Ojaide, Moses Tsenongu, Terhemba Shija, Onoome Okome and Emman Usman Shehu argue that the language of poetry has to be simple in order to embrace large audiences. On the other hands, critics and writers such as Titi Adepitan, Obakanse S. Lakanse and Maik Nwosu have decried the declining nature of literary language especially among the poets who feel they are so much burdened with social messages that aesthetic embellishment is an unnecessary luxury for a poetry that must convey the pains and anguish of the people in the society. Adepitan's contention is that "even social commentaries need some polish, some skills, and there can't be much to admire in it when it becomes an invitation to all comers who think they have 'a message'" (125). Raji's position is made clear when he says, in an interview with Segun Ajayi, that "[a]s much as I try to address the ordinary man in the street, I also try to couch my language in beautiful and elevated style without dancing towards obscurity. If there is what you can call a meeting point between the pedestrian and [the] highfalutin, I try to work in-between the two" (3). How Raji achieves this is by deploying metaphors that are not difficult to fathom but are not simplistic in their linguistic and sensuous constructs. The following passage, taken from song XII of *Lovesong*, demonstrates the accessibility and the tendency to appeal, which is common to the construction of images in Raji's poetry:

> The ones who came before had sweeter passions
> They milked the mule of her mirth
> And left us the hide and the rind
> And a yawning question on patriotism
> Just a little garlic on gaping sores...

The image of a people milking the best out of a mule is clear. Similarly, the metaphorisation of "the hide and the rind" as well as 'yawning" does not pose any obscurity for an average reader. In positioning his language and style within the middle ground between complexity and simplicity, Raji achieves an eloquence that draws audiences to his poetry and nudges such audiences towards a mental activity required to fully appreciate the condensed language of poetry.

Since the theme often foregrounds the image, and since Raji's themes are mostly political, presenting the plight of the masses and the cruelty of those who cause the suffering, the images are mostly unpleasant in the sense that they are conjured to evoke in the reader sympathy for the masses and hostility towards the oppressors. Raji, through his imagery, attempts to present very clear pictures of oppression. A very common feature in Raji's deployment of imagery is the use of animals to represent the oppressor-figure. In *Webs of Remembrance*, easily his most engaging poetry collection, you find such images staring at you: "i see rodents still / i see reptiles in new skins / i see bats flying above the flood" (23-25). Rodents and reptiles are known to human beings as destructive animals; bats are known for their deceptive physiology – not completely birds and not completely four-footed animals. Raji's symbolism means that a dictator, whether military or civilian, is as destructive as the rodent who only comes to steal and destroy; like the reptile whose bite is poisonous and can kill; and like bat that defies clear classification among animals. In "Silence II" (*Webs of Remembrance*), Raji begins by saying "Who sings when the Beast prowls". The image of the restless beast refers to the oppressor having his stooges all around the nation, looking for both real and imagined detractors. In another poem, "An underground poem", Raji also refers to the oppressor and his men as "chameleon and castrated dogs" (12). One of Raji's engaging images is found in "Love song" (*A Harvest*) where he says:

> When Love spoke
> I became a rebel of the blood
> in a convent of scorpions
> without a sting to call my own. (13-16)

Scorpions represent the oppressor and his cohorts. The nation becomes their "convent" as soon as they take it through coup. The persona is moved by his love of people, his society, to become a rebel in this convent. While such representations of the oppressor in heinous animals run through Raji's corpus, let it be pointed out that it is not particular to his poetry alone because most of the poets, including older poets such as Niyi Osundare and Odia Ofeimun, who wrote under and about the military era in Nigeria deploy such animals to illuminate the nature of the oppressor. In her *Comparative Studies in African Dirge Poetry*, GMT Emezue points out that the new poets use such images because their poetry largely laments, meaning that "[the] tendency to load enemy with all kinds of negative images has become a continuing tradition with most poetry of lamentation" (133).

Raji prunes his images, giving a sense of purity and clarity. This is why Osundare talks of the "limpidity" of his imagery ("Soyinka and the New Generation" 4). This requires skills in using words, which Raji possesses judging from his poetic output. Consider this example from "Endless wondering" (*A Harvest*) where he refers to the beauty of a woman: "are you the bronze / among crooked woods / sculpted only by God's chisel hands" (9-11). Here a picture, unstained, is presented of a beautiful woodwork created by the arch-creator. Referring to the greatness of the Library of Congress, Raji writes, (in *Shuttlesongs: America*, 62),

> I sought my fancy in Romanesque parks
> in the futuristic bowels of archives
> and the boundless fountains
> of the Library of Congress.

The use of the metaphors "bowels" and "fountains" to create the image of depth, vastness and greatness is part of the special skills the poet has in choosing the appropriate words to paint a picture for the reader. Consider these images of (sexual) intercourse, de-vulgarised, rather innocuous, but penetrative:

> i want to do to you what needles of rain do to the parched earth
> i want to do to you what the morning sun does to butter nuggets
> what the honey does to the pollen in the shrub
> i want to hide in you, and hide you in me. (*Gather My Blood*, 132)

The metaphors are those of intercourse that result in reproduction. When the rain meets the parched earth, fertility takes place. Sunshine beautifies and nourishes butter nuggets; and the relationship between honey and pollen is obvious to us.

Personification abounds in Raji's poetry. On page 41 of *Shuttlesongs: America*, Raji, describing the scenery of New York, says, "The Road will break / The boulevard will bow / There is no pain of panting / Through the million throng". Quite visible in these lines dominated by personification is the action of "bow" that "boulevard" performs. When in the prologue of *Lovesong*, Raji says, "but I cannot run away from the lashes of History," the personification is not only clearly put, but it also explains itself. When people fail to learn from their history, they get "lashed" by the history. In "The mutineer's song" (*Webs of Remembrance*), Raji begins by saying, "Let the skies cry in crimson rage I shall not flee". Since the skies are not living things, it is only metaphorical that they can cry. And in "Orphan cry", the poet, in the beginning of the poem, writes, "a generation of thorns tickles my skin", and goes on to say, "a generation of spears peels my flesh". These are figurative expressions meant to reinforce the incisiveness of the persona's feeling towards external oppression.

In most cases, the poet uses apostrophe to address the oppressor or the oppressed that is not physically in existence. Some poems, covertly animistic, like "Farewell to myth I" (*Webs of Remembrance*), run all through as apostrophes. In "Farewell to myth I", Raji addresses the god, Olokun, railing against it for its unconcerned attitude towards those who are suffering in its land. The poem opens thus:

> Where are you, o Olokun
> They rape you and raid your children
> They march on your fertile brows
> And rid gods of crude pain in your veins

Also in "Farewell to myth II" (*Webs of Remembrance*), Raji, with an enraged tone, says, "Go up in flames, dear goddess". The same technique is deployed in "For dead gods" (*Webs of Remembrance*). We find another example of personification in "Rain song" (*A Harvest*), where Raji, in a rare sense of romanticism, says,

> There's a blue eagerness in the loin of clouds

The wind is pregnant
With seductive memories
Of burning flesh, of pollen laughters.

Clouds and wind are given human attributes to foreground their usefulness to life, given the fertility of the soil that comes with the rainy season.

Other literary devices that a keen reader can discern in Raji's poetic embellishment include irony, sarcasm, paradox, oxymoron, antithesis, hyperbole, synecdoche, metonymy and literary allusion. For instance, on page 41 of *Shuttlesongs: America*, Raji makes allusion to Ralph Ellison's *Invisible Man* where he writes, "Sometimes too / You're invisible like Ellison's man / Nobody cares if you're white, black / or both or neither". T. S. Eliot echoes loudly in Raji's fourth volume of poetry: *Lovesong for My Wasteland*. It calls to mind Eliot's "Lovesong of Alfred J. Prufrock" and "Wasteland."

As a poet with a distinct sense of musicality, Raji pays close attention to sound effects in his versification. Raji's poetry, in terms of musicality, evidences Walter Pater's declaration that poetry "constantly aspires to the condition of music" (quoted in Egudu 53); or Paul Valery's description of the Symbolist Movement that its chief task was "to take back from music what poets had lost to it" (quoted in Bowra 9). Alliteration is primal to Raji's sense of musicality. In *Webs of Remembrance*, we encounter such alliteratively designed lines as "I belong to no bacchanal / babel of Goddam gods" ("An underground poem", 24); or this conscious alliterative listing: "Burutu-Bori-Babe-Beniboye-Benisaide" ("Farewell to myth I", *Webs of Remembrance*), which are the names of towns that are environmentally degraded in the Niger Delta of Nigeria. A reader will encounter repetition in almost all of Raji's poems. The repetition of "which" in the extract below brings out the kind of cadence one often sees in Raji's poetry:

My song is half the wit
Which bakes the bread
Which breaks the fast

Which feeds the barren land
(Song XXIV, *Lovesong*).

Apart from repetition, Raji deploys parallelism to achieve musicality as the example below shows:

What will earth say to the toxin?
What will the deer say to the hunter?
What will the elephant say to the poacher?
What will the woodpecker say to the sawmiller?

In these parallelistic questions are irony and paradox, which depict the extent of system failure in a society. As the instances above show, there are other sound effects such as assonance and consonance.

Raji who began his art with singing in the Yoruba language is one of the poets writing in Nigeria today whose craft cannot be removed from the domain of the Yoruba orature. The concept for Raji's first collection of poetry, *A Harvest of Laughters* is taken from Yoruba's wisdom surrounding the phenomenon of laughter. Raji explains this in his introduction to the collection:

From my life and others, I'd want to affirm the potable necessity and the therapeutic force of laughter. As the Yoruba say, "Erin ko yato, titi to fi de `lu oyinbo" (Laughter is uniform, from here to the whiteman's land). It strikes an impressionist universal current, like instrumental music, between cultures, races and the sexes. (10)

All through the collection, Raji who sees laughter as "the rainbow paste on weeping scars," thematises the force laughter has of lifting one from the suffering one encounters daily as a result of leadership failure in Nigeria. He thus offers the masses hope through laughter. Similarly, in *Shuttlesongs: America*, Raji takes a concept from the Yoruba traditional religion in the design of the cover of the book. In an interview with this researcher, he explains thus:

you look at the image of the Statue of Liberty that you

think is on the cover. But it is not. It is the image of an African woman, carrying the insignia of Sango, the Yoruba god of thunder and lightning. And then you see the impression of the Middle Passage, of boats, ships, conveying people across the ocean. Behind that you find the pocket of huts representing the different West African kingdoms, where people were taken to the New World. And that spreads over to the back of the book. But the first thing that an unsuspecting reader will see that will invite him, or distract him, or infuriate him is the American colour, which is not! (*In Their Voices and* Visions, 74-91)

It is only a poet who is conscious of his roots that will domesticate such imagination as Raji has done. In versifying about his lonely birthday in the US, Raji, in the same volume, uses the popular Abiku spirit in Yorubaland to imagise the eternity of his origin and history. He begins by saying, "Spirit unto spirit, I waited on my / mother's song / Even if I lived forty years more, these / scars will never fade". Here, he likens the scars in his history, i.e. the experience of slavery and oppression to the scars made on *abiku* child to identify it from normal children. The import of this is that anywhere a black African goes his history of slavery serves to unite him with other black Africans. There is therefore a sense in which a common adversity can unite a people.

In most cases, speech wisdom in Yorubaland, nay in Africa, is found running through Raji's poetry. When in "Salutation" (*Webs of Remembrance*) Raji writes,

I salute the song I salute the singer
I salute the patience of quick proverbs
I salute the craft in immortal songs
I salute the pebbles I salute the pearls...

We see not just the musical rhythm of Yoruba orature but also the speech wisdom of the Yoruba people. In "Elegy for towncriers" (*Webs of Remembrance*), Raji uses the onomatopoeic "Yee pa ri pa!" (1), which is an occult greeting among the Ogboni confraternity of Yorubaland. In "The Agidigbo speaks volume"(*Webs of Remembrance*), Raji idiomatises "agidigbo", a Yoruba drum noted for its speech quality. It is the drum of the elderly ones who, at the height of their wisdom, only speak in proverbs; it is, in fact, a kind of philosopher's drum that radiates wisdom which only the wise do understand. As universalised as the vision of *Lovesong* is, the craft of the volume is rooted in Yoruba tradition. The running imagery of farmer, farming and harvest; the reference to Yoruba items such as *olukondo* (an epithet for a small sharp knife used by the guild of circumcisers in Yorubaland); and such proverbial statements as "When the hour of hunger descends on the homestead / Then the farmers talk of rains long imagined", all attest to Raji's sense of artistic domestication. Furthermore, they reinforce the need for the poet to discover his roots, as Christopher Okigbo has done in his poetry, before he is able to rise against the social maladies of his nation.

This work undertakes a critical study of Raji's poetry principally to dwell on the thematic issues and explore its unique imagery. Raji's images, especially those that present sharp pictures of bad leadership, oppression and plunder in his land, his lover, are enchanting because they are acute and incisive and have remained "the most potent tool for him to affect the emotions of his audience" (Udoeyop 152). The advantage this study has is that it makes an in-depth exploration of Raji's poetry, mostly from the standpoints of the personas. Tanure Ojaide, in his study of Soyinka's poetry, rightly points out, "the critic who focuses upon the poet's persona can provide a more comprehensive treatment of the poems. The persona unites all the poems the poet writes" (*The Poetry of Wole Soyinka*, 3). Out of this unity emerges Raji's sharp vision powered by an engaging motif in the metaphor of laughter.

**Notes**

1. There has been a debate on whether it is right to refer to this generation of Nigerian writers as the third generation or not. A school headed by Harry Garuba thinks that, given the

emphasis on modern Nigerian writers, this generation is the third. On the other hand, another school, led by Obiwu, thinks that for a proper historiography of Nigerian literature, this generation is not the third generation but the fifth. For a proper understanding of the arguments of the two schools, see Harry Garuba's "The Unbearable Lightness of Being: Re-figuring Trends in Recent Nigerian Poetry." *English in Africa*. 32. 1. (2005): 51-72; and Obiwu's "The History of Nigerian Literature, 1772-2006." *Farafina*. 7. (2006). Our position here is that if "modern" and "in English" are used as a prefix and a suffix to "Nigerian literature" respectively, then this generation is the third.

2.   General Ibrahim Badamasi Babangida ruled Nigeria as a military Head of State and later as a President from 1985 to 1993; and late General Sani Abacha ruled Nigeria as a military Head of State from 1993 to 1998. Their regimes are said to be the worst dictatorships that Nigeria has ever witnessed.

3.   The article appeared in *African Literature Today*, Vol. 1-4, 1972.

4.   In an interview I had with Raji (see In *Their Voices and Visions*, 74-91), he explained elaborately the influence of the Yoruba traditional songs on his poetry.

5.   See Jean-Paul Sartre's book *What is Literature?* And for an insightful critique of Sartre's theory of literature, see, among others, David Caroll (67-90).

6.   There is evidently a difference, in matters of diction, between the language of a poem and that of a song. For a good explication of this difference, see Odia Ofeimun's interview titled "Truth and the Language of Poetry" published in *Prism*, vol. 1, no. 1, 2001.

7.   His early poetry refers to the poems collected in *A Harvest of Laughters* (1997) and *Webs of Remembrance* (2000); and his later poetry refers to the volumes: *Shuttlesongs: America – A Poetic Guided Tour* (2003), *Lovesong for My Wasteland* (2006) and *Gather My Blood Rivers of Song* (2009). There is, I have argued now and then, a technical lacuna between the early poetry and the later poetry. Raji admits this and he offers his sensitivity to his audience as the impulse for that.

# CHAPTER

# 2

As we have earlier noted, Remi Raji is a poet who consciously locates himself and his art in the dominant literary tradition in Africa. This seems a natural thing to do but we are also aware of poets, even within Raji's generation, who move or desire to move against the tide of tradition, and seek to carve out for themselves a personal, hyper-artistic sphere in the fulfilment of their artistic vision. Uche Nduka, given his overwhelming formalism, is obviously one of such poets; and recently Ismail Bala Garba, Ahmed Maiwada and Gimba Kakanda have emerged as poets with techniques that seek to deviate from mainstream tradition of African poetry, although their perceived uniqueness is arguably a re-enactment of the so-called euro-modernist tradition. Raji is incurably a political poet, extremely socialist in tone and, as we have in his own words pointed out, he deliberately connects his poetry to the question of nationhood. In this chapter we will look at Raji's process of self-inscription in Africa's dominant literary tradition, and his fashioning of an artistic vision anchored on an aesthetic of rage in accordance with the protest nature of African literature. Raji patently typifies the angry poet of his age, an age that Niyi Osundare, elsewhere, has called the angry generation.[1]

## Self-Definition: Roots, Creeds, Strategic Metaphors
Like some of his contemporaries on the scene today, Raji is conscious of his role as a poet of his nation and in his poetry he often defines himself and his duty.[2] He knows of the peculiarities of the writer especially as essentialised in his ideological stand. This definition is thus not only that of the self, but that of other

writers too; those often collectivised by common poetic root and creed. In some poems where Raji dwells on the travails and triumphs of writers, such as "Duty" (in *Webs of Remembrance*), we see him belonging to that clan of writers whose sympathies for one another is easily a subject of poetry. In doing this, Raji is following the trend that has existed among poets and writers since the beginning of modern written literature in Africa. Great minds in written African literature such as Christopher Okigbo, Wole Soyinka, Chinua Achebe, Dennis Brutus, Kofi Awoonor and Lenrie Peters have had occasions to define themselves as artists against the background of their socialist artistic vision, and the trajectories of critical canons on their works have often tended to be influenced by such self-definition.[3]

Raji's self-definition is largely predicated on his social commitment as a poet. Because he believes that a poet in connecting his art to nationalism must rise beyond the self-glorification of artistry to embrace a "social function" to which true art must lend itself (see Nnolim "African Literature in the 21st Century", 2), Raji crafts imagery and symbolism through which he launches his poetic vision. In *A Harvest of Laughters* and *Shuttlesongs: America*, he refers to himself as "a namesake of laughter." Indeed, Raji, in his corpus, sees laughter as a trope he uses to reach the common people on whose faces sorrow and sadness are etched. In *A Harvest of Laughters,* we encounter Raji as a poet equipped with the knowledge of "the therapeutic force of laughter" (Raji 9) to guard the masses through the harsh realities of the socio-political and economic problems of their land. As a poet who understands "the interplay of social forces, the plenum of forces in continuous tension within his socio-political reality and how he harnesses his talent to react to these forces" (Nwankwo 27), Raji's poetic vision seeks to offer succour to the less privileged ones in his society. A self-proclaimed singer for the masses, Raji's political poems reveal the self-important stance of the poet against the ills of his society. Needless to say that in the era of political poetry Raji belongs to, poetry is reduced to intellectual songs and poets see themselves as singers, "in a way that a popular song writer does not" (Ofeimun 22). The singer is ecstatic, bold and courageous in weaving words against the bad leadership of his land. He has chosen to speak in the face of tyranny. The singing of the songs, itself, is therapeutic for the poet because the songs seem bottled up in him for quite some time and now burst out of him with natural rhythms.

"Introits" is the first poem in *A Harvest of Laughters*, very short and heavy with the metaphor of laughter. It is worth quoting wholly here:

> I will spread my song
> in a sunlight of webs
> I'll seize upon the lemon-smell of laughter;
> No, not for me the twilight tales
> of sick knights
> not for me, the wilting metaphors
> of pain-wrights.

The singer insists on singing despite the "twilight tales" (4) from the "sick knights" (5) which are not only capable of removing his songs from his lips but also his laughter. He is out to explore the therapy that laughter offers and he is doing this not only for himself but for others too. He will ignore the "pain-wrights" (7) because his song through which he is sending forth the "lemon-smell of laughter" (3) will definitely confront the frowns, the worries, common in the land. Laughter is thus the first and recurrent metaphor with which he identifies; and, in doing so, he confers certain symbolic effect on what we ordinarily know as laughter. But there is a sense in which one may problematise Raji's conception of laughter as a therapy. It is contestable to conclude that people who are suffering from oppression should learn to laugh in order to survive the hardship, or that the poet charging against gun-totting soldiers should wear laughter as his armament; it seems to signal docility and inaction. One may not be hasty in interrogating Raji along this line because, as is clear in his poetry, the laughter he prescribes is not the one that comes from a passive people but from a people actively engaged in their own emancipation. The issue here is that of signifying, what Henry Louis Gates Jr., in his theory of the Signifying Monkey refers to as "the trope of tropes" (286), the wily deployment of a language, often in total disregard of its denotative representation, to reach a goal. Indeed Raji emerges, with his *confrontational* laughter, as the Esu figure of the Yoruba mythology, a "master of style and the stylus" (Gates 287) with which he can take the position of the monkey "who speaks *figuratively*, in a symbolic code" (Gates 289) against the lion.

But the poet Raji is quite combatant in his tone, often throwing caution to the wind when hurling invectives at the oppressor.[4] He creates diverse personas who believe in and emphasise the might of the poet in effectively conquering the oppressor. For instance in "Gift" (in *A Harvest of Laughters*), a short poem written in run-on lines, the poet-persona reveals his strength and weapons. He announces, perhaps proudly, that "The chameleon has given me the gift / of a thousand garbs" (1-2). What this means is that whichever way or side his enemy attempts to strike, he is ready to dodge. In fact, he will elude his opponents. He considers himself imbued with spider's "contraptions" (5), equipped with the tortoise's "wisdom" (8), filled with the songbird's "beaded tales" (11) and fully, combatively emboldened to

> ...rise now
> hand in hand with Memory
> holding my frowns in fragments of laughter. (18-20)

The last, oxymoronic line summarises the therapy of laughter upon the sorrows and worries of life because frowns are symbolic of the unpleasantness of life that is directly antithetical to laughter. Notice, however, that he chooses the clever way, like the quintessential clever hair that will outsmart the lion. The mutation of his mien from frown to laughter paradoxically portrays his signifying attempt to attack those who are responsible for creating worries in the land, and an assured optimism that he will win the fight. In this paradox we see a balance between oppression and optimism which turns out to be a forte for Raji in his examination of the current state of anomie and his persistent recognition of a bright future ahead of this state. Raji also defines himself, unveils his strategy, in the first poem of *Webs of Remembrance*, "Salutation", where he comes alone, unannounced, "gently / Like the evening rain" (1-2) and "in silence / Like the dews of a virgin morn" (3-4). You will wonder what this gentle and silent fighter can do in the crises of misrule he is venturing into. Then "suddenly / Like thunder, like the rain at noon," (5-6), he springs up, battle ready. The poems that follow, in that collection, mostly concretised on the imagery of brutality against the innocent, of the bestiality of the oppressor, point to the resilience, the courage, and the arrogance of the poet against the leaders that rather than build the nation have plundered it. The picture Raji presents to us is that of a poet who is battle ready and will not mince words in calling a spade a spade. Like most poets on the scene today, that is what Raji has chosen to be.

In *Lovesong*, the poet-singer calls our attention to himself in "I WAS A VICTIM BEFORE I BECAME A CYNIC" (these capitals and subsequent ones are his). It means he does not give in to the oppression of the moment. His cynical posture now is because he is patriotic about the fate of his land. His patriotism, as a result of which he now sings, ushers him into a realm of optimism in which

> The day [is] brighter where there was once darkness
> Love spelt in the colours of the rainbow
> where the hardness of hatred used to rule. (3-5)

Despite this optimism, the singer-persona is aware that all is not totally well with his nation, since people are still afraid of the "acid rain" (6). Then he goes ahead to reiterate the vicarious duty he has chosen for himself. The fear that has powered him to begin this song is "the father's [fear] for the future of his children" (9). He is concerned about the future; only those who look at the future with such concern are patriotic. While patriotism is part of every poet's sensibility, only few poets have artistically articulated their patriotism in Nigerian poetry like Raji, in what he sees as his "nationalist imagination". The essence of Raji's self-definition is to identify himself, as a poet, with those who are suffering in the land. Beyond that, however, he defines the kind of powers he has brought to the battleground with which he will effectively launch his attack on those he feels have incurred the wrath of the poet and, by extension, the wrath of the masses.

This self-definition is an attempt to construct a personal idiom. Whether Raji's idiom is unique or not it effectively locates his artistic vision in the literary tradition of African protest writing. He chooses to tread the path that has been trodden by many, which is still being trodden, not because others have trodden it but because it is a path a writer primarily concerned with literature as instrumentation for cultural struggle and social change must tread.

## Tension and Intention: The Aesthetics of Rage

The poet's (self-)righteous anger against the failings of his society expressed in his art is what Raji himself has elsewhere couched "aesthetics of rage". It is what galvanises the poetic vision behind his poetry and defines his duty as a poet. The poet, as Saleh Abdu points out, has to make a choice "between the Establishment and the People" (xiv), and it is to the plight of the people that Raji lends his voice. Raji does so with a certain artistic temper as we will see in the poems discussed here. The poet is moved with passion and rage to state the suffering of the masses and goes further to attack those responsible for their suffering. He is following the steps of the poets of the Alter-Native tradition.[5]

In "I Rise Now" (*A Harvest of Laughters*), the poet details his treatise in the artistic act of seizing "upon the lemon-smell of laughter" ("introit" in *Webs of Remembrance*) to confront the inadequacy of his society. He starts by showing the unpleasant things happening around him which should normally evoke sorrow, not laughter. In surrounding countries, there is "the news of acid rain" (3). This rain is burning the people; it is obvious that they are trapped. The poet goes on to point out that "our harvest tracks" (5) are useless because of "the blighted clouds of a locust train" (6). The "locust train" is a metaphor that captures the successive governments that impoverish Nigeria or, in a wider context, Africa. Hostilities and unnecessary conflicts seethe the land and no one knows peace any more. And because there is no peace,

> Nobody
> no body seems to know
> how to smile again,
>
> not even a grin colours the face. (6-10)

Such is the hardship and cruelty that the ordinary people in the society face. Even the dead as shown in the pun, "no body", do not know peace. Everyone is busy trying to survive in a climate of chaos; there is no time for entertainment, for laughter, because that has become extravagant to Nigerians living in a plundered nation. The imperatives of the society have occasioned "the rash of times / in the bellies of lovers and children" (18-9); the people in the society are engaged in the serious problems of looking for what to survive on, especially with the "acid rain" (3) which may also stand for the ethnic wars that spread in Africa during the middle-and-late-1990s such as the genocide in Rwanda, Somalia and Darfur. Raji situates the deplorable condition of Nigeria in a wider context to remind us of the history of continental violence Nigeria is part of. As if those who have come before the poet have watched the course of violence unchecked, the poet declares:

> I rise today
> to the sunrise sigh
> of beaded words. (25-30)

This is his duty. He is determined, repeatedly re-incarnated to create laughter. He vacuums his brain of "memories of slaving rites" (29) and advances "with long drums of laughter / to slaughter a thousand dragon-dreams of pain" (37-35). The poet's choice to laugh at such time is a phenomenal step towards freeing himself from the grip of socio-political shackles. The tone of the poem is triumphal because the persona seems to have discovered something that is not only more powerful than the problems of his society but is also capable of making nonsense of the problems. And with it he is set about to launch his attack. This is bravery on the part of the poet. Whether or not this brave tone translates to a positive action is a different issue altogether. But what Raji makes evident in this tone phenomenalises the social vision of most African poets. "Bound to Remember" (*Webs of Remembrance*) is an enlightening step into the poet's self-given duty. The first two lines of the poem, repeated as a couplet, carry the destruction of the Nigerian polity by the oppressive leaders which requires his intervention as a poet:

> no water runs where the Niger flows
> no fish swims where the Benue berths. (1-2)

Rivers Niger and Benue suffice for the geographical mapping of Nigeria. They bestride the country and they are, here, symbolic of the immense natural resources the country is blessed with. They are barren, the poet points out, because they do not have water and fish. What is the use of a river without water and fish? In this imagery of useless rivers, Raji captures the total collapse of system in Nigeria. Using a different image to show what Raji has presented here, the British journalist Karl Maier says, "[d]esigned by alien occupiers and abused by army rule for three quarters of its brief life span, the Nigerian state is like a battered... elephant staggering toward abyss with the ground crumbling under its feet" (xx). This makes every patriotic person grieve. That is why the poet goes on to state his grief, which is "long like the rivers" (3). Such is the grief that compels him to rise without fear because he has, unlike other people, chosen to use his poetic imagination for the course. In a confrontational tone, he sees himself as a "thunder in the kidneys of liars" (6). The leaders are liars. They are people who make promises but fail, often intentionally, to keep the promises. The next metaphor is harsher: the poet says he will remember "the necklace of the albatross /

hanging in the *hearts of butchers* (italics added, 9-10). The picture of butchers, weighed down by "the necklace of the albatross," is certainly a strong one. The meaning is unmistakable: the butchers are killers and slayers. Indeed, a great deal of people lost their lives to the unspeakable cruelty of the military dictators. In the next stanza, the poet speaks of the oppressor's "bomb-game goon" (11), referring to the arbitrary eruptions of bomb blasts in the land; of "landmines of lies" (12), referring to the oppressor's despicable lies more destructive than a military weapon; and of "oasis of blood" (13), indicating the senseless waste of human blood in organised killings. These have inflicted such a deep scar on the land that the poet maintains he will not forget nor forgive the evils against his nation. The next image in the poem reduces the human status of the bad leaders. They are "rodents" (23). The rodents, we all know, are good at destroying while searching for food. Raji's metaphor here is quite apt because it captures the greed of our leaders. It shows that the leaders are so senseless in their desire to acquire wealth that they use all kinds of means to cause untold destruction to the system. They are shameless thieves like the rodents. They also destroy after stealing. What follows is the image of "reptiles in new skin" (24). Reptiles are noted for their poison. A dictator does not only carry poison in his mouth, like the reptiles, he also carries it in his actions. He therefore does not hesitate to hit anyone that questions his inhuman actions. Finally, the oppressor is one of the "bats flying above the flood" (25). The bat, by nature, is an ambiguous mammal. While it flies like other birds, it does not appear like a bird physically. No metaphor can better capture the military-civilian nature of self-made presidents that rule the country with orders. Even when civilians come, they are militaristic in nature.

Probably the poem that more strikingly captures the poet's philosophy of struggle is entitled "Duty", dedicated to Odia Ofeimun, one of Nigeria's influential poets. Raji casts his mind on the responsibility of the poet, especially the African poet who versifies with an extra-literary intention. In the first stanza, Raji prescribes that the poet's first duty is "to make love / To language, to land, and to liberty" (1-2). It is expected that the poet distinguishes himself from other craftsmen through the way he weaves words. His major strength is in the way he handles words. Being in love with language calls to mind Ofeimun's assertion that "language ought to move, and the poet...is in a better position to help it move, more than any other kind of performer in words" (24). A poet also has to love his land, because he draws his thematic material from his land; it is the nexus of his nationalist imagination. His land is definitely peopled by men and women who need freedom; hence the poet should not only come to love liberty but should also lead the people towards freedom. That is ultimately the African poet's engagement; and, as Niyi Osundare has pointed out, "[it] is not possible for a conscientious writer not to be engaged" (Interview with Omowunmi Segun, 37). Raji is, here, redefining and reinforcing the forte of the socially engaged writer. Raji becomes more definitive about the language of the poet in the second stanza. The kind of language the poet uses is metaphorical. His metaphors create wisdom to his people, to his generation, addressing all spheres of it ("armpits of Time" (4)). The poet should also be critical of people who hold powers. He checks the consciences of those in power. The poet should, as much as possible, depict the reality as it is. This is what Raji means by the poet evoking "the geography of bleeding images" (7). It is also the poet that can tend the minds of the people, especially the simpletons in the society, who just take things as they come. He has to endeavour to "make fires in bushels of ignorance..." (11). It is when the poet does all the aforementioned that he settles for living "beyond mortal wishes" (12). He has to remain an "eternal kernel of utterance" (13) so that no one, no circumstance can penetrate him easily. Raji believes that a poet is dutiful. "Poetry is about being a watchdog in a moment where there is a lot of chaos," so he says in an interview (Sou'wester, 13). He demonstrates that in this poem.

In "The Critic's Dilemma", Raji moves from the function of

poetry to that of journalism or general writing. This poem is more elaborate because it presents the general apathy the Nigerian society under the military dictators had towards journalists and writers. There were cases of hostility on the part of the government towards the journalists and the masses. Many of them who were brave to live under the heinous regimes often wrote from undercover. This was because, no matter the violence directed against them, they considered it a selfless duty to write in order to take the society out of regression. Most Nigerian journalists, during military dictatorships, understood that "Journalism is not meant to make the environment cosy for leaders of nations; it is to prod them to act in the interest of the larger society" (Onanuga quoted in Ajibade 12). That underscored the guerrilla journalism in Nigeria that helped in enthroning democracy. This is the context for Raji's "The Critic's Dilemma". At the beginning of the poem Raji sees the journalist, the writer, as "Ifa's Acolyte" (1). Ifa is a cultural deity in Yorubaland who is often contacted to reveal the future. It also holds the gospel of truth. Raji's point is that just as the deity safeguards the society by telling the truth that in most cases set the society free from trouble, so does the writer, "by the volume of his narrative "(2). This is the visionary essence of the writer, placing the writer side by side with Orunmila who is the legendary figure behind the Ifa corpus or chants. But the writer has enemies in the society. They are probably those who are not concerned with the development of the land or those mindless of what they can do for the land. They are rather concerned about what they can take from the land. Such people are materialistic in their thinking. They ask the writer:

> Tell us, talkative one
> How many fishes of late
> has your printed pop fetched from the waters of
> Lagos banks?
> How many cowries of oriki have blessed your sweat
> today? (7-10)

The writer lives in a society in which little respect is given to thinkers and philosophers. Once one is able to acquire riches (and it does not matter the way he does so), he commands respect in the society. Hence the writer, who has taken the path of knowledge and thinking like "Plato, Boccacio, Burke to Bathes and Lentricchia" (12), has nothing to show materially. Here, we may recall Pythagoras' theory of the classes of human beings. The sixth century B.C. philosopher postulates that there are three classes of people in every society. The first class, to which the majority belongs, consists of people whose primary interest in the world is to acquire material wealth even if it is at the expense of other people around them. The second class is made up of people whose interest is to acquire fame. People here are, of course, not as many as those in the first class. The third class, which often has the least number of people, has thinkers whose goal in life is to study the universe and suggest ways in which it can be made better. It is in this class that the poet chooses to be. From Raji's portrayal, and in consonance with Pythagoras' classification, the society is a moneyed one as we see in the image of the "trophy in the vault of the Central Bank" (14). But the writer is not hemmed in by the *minty* smell of the moneyed society. He sees dignity and high sense of duty in his craft:

> I am the unstoppable alphabet
> which worries the wind
> the scathing smooth sentence
> which arrests your conscience
> my word startles...
> my word stabs the robber's dreams
> and irrigates the lover's heart. (19-25)

Thus the writer is not only dedicated to his job he is also envisioned. He bears a social vision for his society. Writers, right from the beginning of time, have always seen themselves within this purview. Raji is a poet, like most African writers, who stretches his consciousness of a writer's social vision early defined in "Duty". This often results to what Abdu sees as the disengagement of the poet from narcissism "towards political engagement and partisanship" (ix).

Raji returns to poetry in "The Spirit". Here it is not only the function of poetry, but also the nature of poetry that he focuses on. We have images running in defining poetry. Such images as "what rainfalls drum / into corn-ears of Earth" (13-4) and "what the sunbird sings" (15) bring out the musical nature of poetry. It is natural that this comes from a poet who genuinely believes poetic thoughts be rendered in strong musical qualities. There are also images such as "what riverbeds hide / from wandering eyes" (21-2) and "the monkey's path / in a platoon of twines / and trees" (24-6), depicting the wisdom of figurative language in poetry. The poet uses figures of speech to create images so that even the harshest truth he has to say is dressed euphemistically. For, as Nyong Udoeyop says, "[w]hen the poet's language creates an accurate image, the proper emotions will flow, hopefully, and the health of the society may be saved from deterioration" (148). In essence, the poet does not speak directly, so that his "common lips" (32) can tell "the cruel crown" (32) whatever truth is there to tell. The persona asks for more power to be able to stand as a poet in a cruel society. Poetry, then, becomes a weapon with which the poet can boldly confront the despoilers, and from what we infer from Raji's aesthetics of rage, the poet feels optimistic that his weapon positions him as a victor in this discourse of engagement. "Riddle I" presents a riddling persona who has the tendency to persist, to move despite odds. Beyond the poet's combative stance, we see the usual Rajian optimism running through the images of "salty milk in succulent huts of coconuts "(2); of "evergreen roots, sap and kernel" (4): and of "fronds of flesh and wine / in an oasis of thirst and taste" (5-6). These images show consistency in nature. Stanza three even captures this optimism more:

> I am the riddle of desert rains
> river's course
> fire's foam
> earth's fragrance

wind's breath. (7-11)

The images here present the energies of nature. Desert rains come like succour. A river moves endlessly. Fire's foam (a rather blurry metaphor) shows the indelible marks of fire on anywhere it moves. Generation after generation will continue to feel the fragrance of the earth. They all seem to show immortality, though the poet's concern here is the resilience of a person to live through the hardship of society, unruffled. In these images is evoked the willpower of human beings to persist in spite of oppression. The substances of "labouring lepers" (13) and "mocking hens" (15) as metaphors show that certain persons are responsible for the societal problems. The poet is sure that he will not fail in his endeavour against them. "Riddle II" reinforces and reiterates the poet's duty. The persona who presents himself as a complex riddle becomes more definitive about the people or institutions he stands against. With the use of capital letters, "I AM..." (1), we see the I-am-certainly-greater-than-you nature of the persona which implies he can face whatever situation in the struggles. Like a pugilist, he has a

    ...clenched fist
    itching to break the brows
    of incontinent emperors. (2-4)

The emperors are the military dictators with an inordinate passion to damage the nation. Already, there are "bloody tears / of bruised stones" (6-7) because of the cruelty of those emperors. The poet-persona thus fights them and soothes the pains of their victims. This is one of the poet's services to humanity. He positions himself between the oppressor and the oppressed, invokes destructive thunder on the oppressor and brings tenderness to the oppressed. In stanza three, we see the dictators as "gruesome weeds" (10) under the sharp, cutting blow of the poet-persona who sees himself as capable of conquering them. The poet-persona continues to use the images of bravery, although in the last stanza his stand becomes shaky: "I feel no ease in this riddle of balance" (18).

Raji creates a character that sees himself as a lone fighter who will succeed against the evil of the emperors.

Raji's long-breath poem, *Lovesong for My Wasteland*, which contains forty-five stanzas, symbolic of the forty-five years of Nigeria as an independent State (as at the time it was published), begins with a prologue that is a dramatic poem (or a poetic drama since there are stage directions). The responsibility of the poet is articulated in this drama. The probable point is that a poet does not set out to sing for the sake of singing except induced by an issue that does not only disturb the peace of his land but also of the entire humanity. There are four characters on stage: Gong, Takie, Gambia and Asabi. Gong, whose voice will lengthen into the poet-persona's voice, speaks first and his speech from the outset reveals the thematic direction of the volume. The artist of the selfless duty we often see in Raji comes out clearly in the first stanza:

> People of the land, the living and the dead,
> those today whose lives count for nothing
> and those tomorrow who would live as if
> they have no future, hear me out,
> it is your story I have come to spin
> in the marketplace of thought. Hear me now,
> it is the smell of your history that chokes the
> singer out of silence...(1-8)

Gong sees himself as a singer whose song carries the ups and downs of history and knows fully well the consequences of yesterday's failure. Already, he suffers from the "lashes of History" (13) and he has to speak out, sing aloud "so that our past shall not / overtake our future "(14-5). The nationalist feeling bursts out in those lines, charting a vision that is consistently centred on the plight of a people loved by the poet. Takie, Gambia and Asabi, themselves inhabitants and, probably, victims of those lashes of history challenge him. Gong, to them, is like the self-important gospeller whose head is overblown with the idea of saving the nation from impending calamity. Gambia points out

that they are "in a season fit only for business and leisure" (25)
and that no one is interested in Gong's song. For Takie, Gong is
"disturbing the moment" (20). Asabi sees Gong as a "hungry
historian" (26). We are at once acquainted with the trio of
Gambia, Takie and Asabi as pleasure-seeking people who care
less or nothing about the direction their nation goes. In fact, they
do not know that the land is on a shaky history and may collapse
with them any moment. In Nigeria, where the military emperors
forged a noxious history in their times, there are many people
who live in this history, unconcerned about its fatal consequence.
That in Raji's construction one good character stands in contrast
with three bad ones indicates that the land is regrettably filled
with people who can do little or nothing to liberate the land
because the culture of plunder, waste and hedonism is instilled
in them.

Gong begins to lambaste them subtly for their "absent
imagination" (29) and they start an argument with him. Gong is
worried that such people do not care about their society. They
mock him for taking up a fight that is not his alone or that cannot
be possibly won. Gong reminds them that they cannot afford to
dally with history because it "is the living thing, the *thingness* of
all / our actions and inactions" (48-9). Gong cannot afford to
ignore history and thus carries "the burden of generations in
[his] chest" (52). That he claims to be carrying the burden of
generations makes Gambia want to listen to whatever story he
has. But Takie remains sceptical and asks "why must a hungry
man come and disturb the peace / with stories about History"
(56-7)? To him Gong may be a deceiver since, he admits, the land
is full of stories of fraudsters and thieves, people who tell lies to
deceive other people. Gong seizes on this to let them know that
the land is indeed full of deceitful stories and criminals but that
it is not the land itself that is bad; it is the people living in the land
that are bad. Truth among the people is what is needed for the
land. The poet is set to kindle this truth for the sake of his society's
survival. The argument takes us to destiny, an idea that often

phenomenalises the mediocrity and lack of direction of a people.[6] Pinning this to the Nigerian situation, many Nigerians, even advanced thinkers, have constantly relapsed into the idea that the destiny of Nigeria is to be what it is today; consequently they make no attempt to emancipate her from the persistent crisis. Many pleasure-seeking Nigerians who benefit from the largesse of the dictators at the expense of the ordinary people reject any protest from artistes, writers and activists and preach this kind of destiny. In his aesthetics of rage, the poet rejects this status quo. Gong's questions here are vital:

> Ah I see, you believe in destiny!
> What kind of destiny do you believe in?
> The one which devours dream? The one which nurtures
> the imagination of the labourer? Or the one which
> glorifies the laziness of the ruler and the rich? (78-82)

While Gambia and others are still thinking of an answer that will definitely demean their sensibilities, Gong goes ahead to tell them the kind of destiny they need to possess in order to emancipate themselves from the lashes of history:

> .... a people's destiny is the weapon in their hands,
> the zeal in their collective soul, the enthusiasm
> on the battlefield
> and the power to tinker with their futures
> by engaging the past in deep dialogue. (84-88)

Gong disarms the trio with this postulation. Asabi wonders if "this one is real" (89) and Takie, still sceptical, thinks it is a waste of time listening to "familiar monologues" (95). Gong insists they have to listen to the song-story because they will definitely tell it to their children one day. Beyond listening, they have to participate in the song-story because, as Gong says,

> Together we shall grow, learning new ways to take
> after years of meandering through self-inflicted labyrinths
> of violence, ignorance, doubt, and despair,

lethargy, deception, corruption, nepotism. (110-114)

The poet's duty, as is shown here, is to lead the people out of the crises of the state. It is at this point that the argument ends. The trio is now interested in knowing who Gong is. In revealing himself, Gong traces a history of plunder and waste in the land.

Raji captures first the years of "impossible flamboyance" (122) which reminds us of the years of General Yakubu Gowon's regime during which it was theorised that the problem of Nigeria was not how to get money but how to spend it. Each soldier, each civilian, came to know the joy and fulfilment of flamboyance. Those years gave way to the Nigerian civil war as Raji shows in these lines:

> when the smokescreen of a failed union gave birth
> to cries of war, and wars.
> Soon, and so suddenly
> music was made out of the skull of men.
> I was born in the year of blood. (125-129)

Then it was the year of "the Wolf" (130), a significant metaphor for the military. Raji has already become adept in equating sharp metaphors to the personalities of the military dictators. "In the year of the Wolf, all that was saved became food / for phantoms and bandits" (133-4). He refers to the soldiers as "warriors who never won a war" (136). Then it is the year of the "Dog" (142). This year belongs to the mindless politicians whose primary aims for hopping into powers are to acquire ill-gotten wealth. The politicians all bark for change: "Change!! One Country!! Change!!! One destiny!!!" (145). The change is never achieved because the change is never really desired. What follows is that

> Sweet dreams became the handle
> of every man who knew the big man in the toilet of
> power. (148-149)

Poverty hits the land and all except those who are in power become victims of the poverty the poet speaks of. After the period of failed politicians (which one can conveniently suggest is the "Second Republic" in Nigeria), a set of supreme military officers, with loud noise of messianism, enters the scene. This is what Gong refers to as "the year of Hyena / which was also the year of Leprosy" (155-6). This period in Nigerian history witnessed the highest degree of mindless oppression unleashed on the common people. The regimes of General Babangida and late General Abacha were the terrible realities of the period. Many people were frightened into exile because those dictators had fearful ways of dealing with their real and imagined detractors and so

> The land became colourful in silence,
> heavy with the breathing only of the Hyena,
> his henchmen, his concubines and their bastard children...
> (165-167)

This is the kind of condition responsible for the waste in the land and Gong, as a singer, is determined to see that such condition does not pass unmentioned. Takie, Gambia and Asabi have softened to the logic of the singer. They now know him. In fact, they know of the years he has spoken of because they have lived through them. Gong concludes so metaphorically, "I can smell your blood in my blood" (174). Here is the thing that links the poet to his nation and pushes the poet to evolve his own discourse of nationalism. Gambia confesses his ignorance for not understanding what Gong does. The trio realise themselves and are won to Gong's side of the argument. Their duty, which has all along been the poet's duty, in the songs that follow, as Gong says, is that

> If we must re-build, we must talk about the plan,
> the foundation, before speaking about the colour
> of the lintel and the shape of the futuristic windows
> But above all, we must speak about the past

and our romances with death and failure...
The secrets of the future is locked in the past,
and what we do now... (202-208)

This statement of mission is what sets Raji's pen on paper for the songs that follow. Indeed, Raji, as a poet, is worried, just like every clear-headed, patriotic Nigerian, that Nigeria, after spending forty-five years, is yet to learn from its past and tidy its present and pick its way for a positive future. This worry calls for a poetic action.

Not only in the dramatic opening, but also in the twenty-fifth verse Raji raises a question about the usefulness of poem (and a poet) to a nation. The point is the potency of poetry as an instrument for social struggle. "WHAT IS POETRY THEN IF IT CANNOT RAISE A FLOOD?" Poetry must be strong enough, metaphorically harsh enough to break "criminal silence" (5). If metaphors are not strong enough to be "the madness of earthquakes" (7), an image well understood if we picture how an earthquake destroys physical structures, then the poet does not need them. They become useless. What the poet needs is a useful poem with which to hit at the public looters. When Emman Usman Shehu says, "every poem becomes dangerous / the moment I open my loud mouth" (68) he means it is through poems he confronts the establishment. He also means every poet ought to have the artistic and social wherewithal to unsettle the received system of oppression at work in his society. It is what Raji dramatises in this poem. In "THERE CAN BE NO ARGUMENT ON WHERE I STAND", the poet states the reason behind the duty he has chosen for himself. After enumerating the systematic havoc that is unleashed on the land by its leaders, he avers that it is the genuine love he has for his land that has made him loud-mouthed in articulating his duty. Referring to the people who inherited his country from colonial masters, whose inability to nurture it has plunged it into chaos, Raji, the land's lover-poet, accuses thus:

The ones who came before had sweeter passions
They milked the mule of her mirth

And left us the hide and the rind
And a yawning question on patriotism. (4-7)

The image created in the lines above presents a land sapped and abandoned to a younger generation that will certainly encounter difficulty in restoring the dignity of the land. Oil, mineral resources and agriculture: the areas that the country can rely on and become rich are plundered by thieves who frolic about in the corridors of power. The singer-persona's ironic statement that he does not know who are responsible for the plunder only points to the fact that the plunder is perpetrated by a powerful class of the society. In the land today, "What remains are the ruins of laughable idiocies" (26). The persona, in the last part of this verse, likens his protestation to "subversion!" (31). This becomes a duty when he, "at the dawn of a new life" (29), remembers all the evils perpetrated against his land, his lover, and he rises to defend her.

Raji's aesthetic of rage is, as we have seen, anchored on that surpassing affection he has for his land and its people; this translates to a literary intension, formed from the tension in the land, which characterises his art as a part of the larger artistic engagement with social commitment in Africa. His poetry is one demonstration of continuing protest literature in Africa due largely to the persistent, unending social contradictions on the continent.

**Notes**

1. In an essay entitled "Soyinka and the Generation After" published to mark the 70th birth day of Wole Soyinka, Niyi Osundare traces the recent development of Nigerian literature vis-à-vis Soyinka's literary prowess and concludes that the existing generation of Nigerian writers is an angry one due largely to the social issues that confront them.

2. As characteristic of writers of every age, self-definitions and explanations of visions are expressed through either prefaces or creative works that are self-referential. Major poets of Raji's

era, such as Ogaga Ifowodo, Emman Usman Shehu, Maria Ajima, have had to explain their visions in the form of prefaces and define themselves even though what they write conspicuously show their visions as writers.

3. For instance, in a 1965 interview, Christopher Okibgo, one of the most difficult poets in Nigeria, declared, "I don't like writing that is committed" ("Interview with Whitelaw", 33) and went on to see himself as an esoteric voice for the oracle of his land. With such utterances from Okigbo, critics have tended to see his poetry as complex privatist chants.

4. In most cases, this combatant tone comes through in the poetry effortlessly and perhaps unconsciously because of what I may term overthematisation. Poets of the military rule generation – Ogaga Ifowodo, Emman Usman Shehu, Toyin Adewale, and many more – possess this tone even without knowing it.

5. In their theorisation, the poets and writers of the Alter-Native tradition, notably Ofeimun, Osundare, Osofisan and Aiyejina, argue that poetry and literature generally should be removed from the sublime realm and brought to the pedestrian realm for the sake of the masses that constitute their audience. In one of his interviews, Bode Sowande, a dramatist of that tradition, says, "[t]he urgency of the need for a functional theatre is so great that a heavily loaded philosophical stuff is a cheat on society" (quoted in Obafemi, *Contemporary Nigerian Theatre*, 170).

6. What Raji is capturing here is certain self-complacency and lackadaisical attitude that existed during dictatorships in Nigeria whereby some intellectuals and professionals, feeding fat on the generosity of the military dictators, could not talk about the evils of the day while some of them simply withdrew into silence. In her novel, *Everything Good Will Come*, Sefi Atta also points this out when she says, "[it] is amazing that privileged people in Nigeria believe that doing nothing is an option" (263).

# CHAPTER

# 3

Having thus fashioned his idiom, powered by a literary intention that seeks to emancipate his society through art, Remi Raji constructs *potent* images that bear his strong, often compulsive messages. One image after another, through a unifying persona, Raji is clear-headed and persistent; the struggle for him is about uncovering the ineptitude of the military oppressor in his destructive activities on the one hand and about providing an alternative means of survival during repression. Concentrating on his figuration of laughter, a poetic means of signifying he creates for himself, we will in this chapter deconstruct some of Raji's images in which his strong political discourse is condensed. Laughter as Raji's poetic idiom is two-edged: it is used to confront the oppressor and it is also used to offer succour to the oppressed. In this display of a political idiom, Raji comes through as a poet who lives through the soul of his nation. It is difficult, going through these poems, not to see Raji as a Nigeria thrashing about, in defiance, amidst the repressive strokes of a cruel hegemonic power.

***A Harvest of Laughters*: Rising through the Mystery of Laughter**
Raji's debut collection, *A Harvest of Laughters*, at once presents him as a poet of the people. Here, we mean a poet who understands and explores what Nourbese Philip calls "the bond between [the] poet and [his] place" (174), and a poet who, according to Tanure Ojaide, is "an oracle and a healer" (quoted in Anyidoho 6) for his people. Using laughter as a metaphor, which later transforms to a motif in his corpus, Raji's aim is to come between the oppressor

and the oppressed in such a way that he uses laughter to combat the former and uses the same laughter to comfort the latter. He does this by exploring, in his own words, "the rather unacknowledged mystery of laughter [which] is its suprasegmental capability of knowing and expressing without much recourse to metaphors" (*A Harvest*, 10). Laughter is thus the idiom of the poet offered as a connective in the tripartite engagement of the poet, the masses and the oppressor in a dialogue that is both humanising and dehumanising, leaving the poet at the centre of the aesthetic of rage. With diverse personas, the poet combatively explodes against the hardship and suffering in the land, specifically heaping curses and condemnations on those who have caused the hardship and suffering. The remarkable resilience in Raji's voice here is fully developed in his subsequent volumes of poetry.

Raji's conceptualisation of laughter is to a large extent carnivalesque, a perspective from which one can further explore the influence of orality on Raji's poetry. While his figuration of laughter is not unconnected with Yoruba traditional wisdom, laughter is a communal, marketplace phenomenon that falls into the broad aspect of carnival among a people. The Russian theorist Mikhail Bakhtin dwells on laughter from this angle in his work on Rabelais. In *Rabelais and His World*, Bakhtin foregrounds carnival as a spirit of a community which is hardly suppressed by hegemonic powers. The people are gingered by the carnivalesque spirit to make subversive utterances and moves which ordinarily would not be tolerated by powerful institutions. Carnival therefore confers on the people the freedom to express themselves in diverse bodily and theatrical forms. One of such is laughter. According to Bakhtin,

> carnival laughter [...] is, first of all, a festive laughter.
> Therefore it is not an individual reaction to some isolated
> "comic" event. Carnival laughter is the laughter of all the
> people. Second, it is universal in scope; it is directed at
> all and everyone, including the carnival's participants. The

entire world is seen in its droll aspect, in its gay relativity.
Third, this laughter is ambivalent: it is gay, triumphant,
and at the same time mocking, deriding. It asserts and
denies, it buries and revives. (11-12)

Laughter, in Bakhtin's view, can therefore be transgressive. It is
this transgressive power of laughter that Raji focuses his idiom
of laughter on. In *A Harvest*, he enjoins his audience to indulge
with him in a laughter that can undermine the forces of
oppression in the land.

In "Orphan Cry", the persona is an orphan in a hostile society.
He laments and narrates his problem and those of other children
in the society. Using provocative images evoked by "thorns" (2),
"weals" (3) and "spears" (6), Raji depicts the violence that the
society inflicts upon the child-orphan. He lacks, he wants, he is
denied and violated. He experiences all these in his land, seen
through the image of "the crimson cage / of deaf emperors" (9-
10), a vivid representation of the police state into which the
oppressor turns the land. In the second part of the poem, there
are even more tear-provoking images. Using plural personal
pronoun, "our" (18), the persona points out that he is among
many children that are condemned to penury by circumstances.
While he is alive, he can do nothing apart from lamenting the
waste of his fellow children. The children are not only hungry,
they are also, sometimes, consumed by death, as they are
unprotected and vulnerable. He indicts the society for looking
on while the cruelty against children goes on:

I see the loud mirage
of eunuch gods;
I see the locust affection
of tears at mourning time. (19-22)

Since the gods are impotent and cannot protect the children,
societal hawks feed on them. Indeed Raji's message is that the
Nigerian society, under those military dictators, did not consider
children as worthy of living.[1] Since children symbolise the future,

the society kills her future as it kills her children. Yet the persona, though a child-orphan, does not surrender himself to death. He intends to soldier ahead with hope, with that metaphorical laughter which contains his survival instincts:

> I'll walk with the herbalist sun...
> To the wake of roaring dreams,
> I'll seize upon the lemon smell of laughter. (26-8)

The lemon smell is the aroma of life that laughter carries. This optimism is stretched to the fourth part of the poem where the persona seems to mean that despite the empty promises of political leaders and shapers of society, he, as well as others, has "grown beyond the blue lullaby / of silence" (35-6). Here, "blue" seems to be used as a colour of insincerity. Similarly, "scalpel" (39), which in "Black laughter" is destructive to life, becomes constructive to life as the orphan hopes to survive and live on "the rattle-wisdom of scalpel songs" (39).

"Old havocs" gives us a Raji whose satirical swipe is not only targeted against those who use politics to suppress the people but also those who use religion. The first part of the poem reads like a political poem and, somewhat confusedly, as a religious poem. Raji's intentional obscurity seems to blur the line between politics and religion here. The persona, in an invocatory tone, addresses a being, urging the being to take actions that will expose the evils of "monster-priests" (9). You would wonder whether the metaphor of "monster-priests" refers to religious leaders or not, especially as the image of drumming and dancing (characteristic of our modern churches) holds sway over this part of the poem. Earlier, one encounters conquerors, either of political minds or of religious minds, in the following lines: "drum out the dreary livers of conquerors / who preyed on the peace-meal of our flesh" (4-5). But in the seventh stanza of the poem, the picture the poet paints appears more of the military dictators:

> So they stay
> in the frivolous fright and faith of men

they build unending castles
of their second coming. (17-20)

The second coming here may not be of the politicians as we see in the pet philosophies of our both civilian and military leaders, after all.[2] It may be the second coming of Jesus Christ, which the priests and pastors and prophets have used to create "frivolous fright" (16) on the mind of the common people. The second part of the poem is not as ambiguous as the first. It is a direct, uncompromising swipe against religious leaders who feast on the ignorance of their congregation mostly because they are interested in enriching themselves while impoverishing their congregation. The tone here is not invocatory any more. Raji assumes his idiosyncratic tone, which is elaborated in *Webs of Remembrance*; he accuses and attacks. These lines are typical of that Rajian rage:

OOSANLA! ALLAH! HOSANNA!
hollow men with livid faiths
with pleading venoms in golden teeth
cannot smell their chaos in the piss of rain. (34-7)

The poet is not against God or religion and by no way blasphemes. He is lambasting the "hollow men" (35) who have bastardised religion for their selfish ends. The second to the last stanza shows Raji's distaste for religious crises as he watches "fools walk stilts while the earth quakes" (47). Raji's indictment of religion in the time of bad leadership is appropriate because that time coincided with the proliferation of churches and hypocritical evangelism in Nigeria. Chimamanda Ngozi Adichie engagingly explores this issue in her first novel, *Purple Hibiscus*, in which she dramatises oppression, caused by religious fanaticism, at a micro level, which, in her views, leads to oppression at a macro level in the society.[3]

In the first four poems of the section captured "Songs of Experience", Raji idiomatises silence. It becomes prominent as an image of suppression or cowardice. In "Silence", the poem that opens this section, Raji, like Okey Ndibe in *Arrows of Rain*, picks the Soyinkan wisdom of the man being dead in him who keeps silent in the face of oppression.[4] But, unlike Soyinka, Raji does not hold acid contempt against the people for keeping silent, though his sneering question here indicts those who keep silent:

    Silence,
    the blue-black lip-
    stick of fear
    or what? (36-9)

The import of Raji's image here is that fear is a lipstick that when the people paint their mouths with they become objects of silence. They are silent because they are afraid. Fear is the conspicuous decoration of silence among the people especially during the dehumanising regimes of the military dictators in Nigeria. The ironic twist in Raji's philosophic thrust is that to be silent and inactive is a cheat on the society, for, as Kofi Anyidoho puts it, "through silence and inaction, a whole community becomes implicated in the terrors of oppression" (4). Earlier, in a refrain, the poet claims that "I know the colour of your silence" (1) and goes on to point out what the colour symbolises. The poet discerns "dark" (2), "red" (13) and "yellow" (22) colours which when mixed may give "the blue-black" colour of fear. We encounter laughter in this poem, but not the kind of laughter that is therapeutic. It is "the beautiful laughters / of others at other people's pain" (34-5). Raji's contextualisation of laughter makes it elastic in a way that different facets of meaning surrounding laughter are explored, manoeuvred and deployed. Whether or not laughter by its texture, context, functionality and attendant symbolism is worth Raji's theorisation here is an issue that is debatable. What laughter means to Raji is not what it may mean to other people. Hence his philosophy of laughter as therapy, on one hand, and as an indicator of sadism, on the other hand, is privatist and challengeable. The next poem "Silence II" is more successful with images. Here, Raji centres the oppressor's cruelty on singing – a professional activity of the artist, the poet. It is the singer or poet who is blessed with the special skill and a highly powered conscience to ideologise his position against the bad leaders. The question, "who sings when the Beast prowls "(1), repeated in the last line of the poem, in capital letters for emphasis, bears the endemic fear instilled in not only the masses of the land but also in the artists, the poets, the intellectuals and the philosophers. One of the major devices of the African dictators is to create a police state in order to arrest the people's consciences. The writer often finds himself the victim of this device. Narrating his experience in an essay entitled "Containing Cockroaches", Jack Mapanje, the repeatedly incarcerated Malawian poet, points out that "[y]ou did not need to commit a crime to be arrested. Being in the limelight was sufficient" (47). This is because the dictator assumes the image of the beast that seeks with inordinate passion those that it can devour:

> when Night thickens
> with dreams of blood
> when Sorrow's scent suffocates
> the remains of lean laughter. (2-5)

"Night" and "Sorrow" have capital initials. This draws our attention to their semantic meanings enlarged from what we know of them. Those two words are also semantically linked to "BEAST" (16) in a paradigm that is obvious to us. The beast moves in the "Night" and when it does so it causes "Sorrow" to human beings. Raji's image of the dictator here is quite incisive. Images that show military oppression stare at us as we read the poem:

> who sings
> when rhyme's winds
> run amok
> like amputated tongues
> when boots barrels
> and the gift of grenades
> chase the choir into silence. (9-15)

The beast is the dictator, the godfather. The "boots barrels" (13) are the soldiers that are at his disposal whom he uses to unleash brutalities on the masses. During the reign of the maximum military ruler, late General Abacha, in Nigeria, real and imagined opposing voices (and artists' voices) were muffled. In his book, *The Last 100 Days of Abacha*, Olusegun Adeniyi reveals the brutality of that regime when he says,

> Security forces committed extra-judicial killings and used excessive force to quell anti-government protests as well as to combat crime, resulting in the death and injury of many individuals, including innocent civilians. Security forces tortured and beat suspects and detainees. (57)

Such brutality is brought upon writers, artists and journalists as well as social activists who dare to raise their voices against the evils of the dictator. The poet laments that the land is barren and dry as a result of this cruelty, for it is the artist, the singer, the writer, who fertilises the land with his fresh, creative output. With a beast that silences the choir of singers, blessed voices of nature, the land is denied of its "remains of lean laughter" (5).

In "Anthem of Silence", Raji focuses on the dictator. There is an imperative command to be silent because "The old emperor is in court" (2) where he does not only feed on "curse-words" (3), words that he uses to oppress the common people, but also dishes then out:

> Waste the widows.
> Maim the maidens.
> Yoke the young
> with (the) muzzles
> of labouring years.
> Let the old lie
> cold in the sunless
> mist of the morning. (5-12)

The dictator, the poet tries to show here, orders for the torture and the killing of the people at will. He blesses when he is, in fact, cursing. He brings "locusts" (15) and "vultures" (20) to plunder the land. He does all these in his drunken state as a dictator because the people have done him nothing to deserve this wrath he unleashes on them. As in "Silence", the poet, in a sneering tone, points out that it is on a people "who have embraced silence" (35) that the dictator rains the "curse-words" (2). On the other hand, like Soyinka's "Chimes of Silence", in which the poet depicts his intense solitude and longing, Raji establishes the state of oppression victims undergo when they are confined to prison. The poet speaks with the voice of the oppressed masses in the next poem, "On Behalf of Silence." The poem, though short, is written in two parts. The persona (in the voice of the masses) laments as well as asserts his allegiance to his fatherland. The masses are aware that they live in "tropics of hunger" (2) and thus their stomachs are "filled / with howling airs, ruled by hurricanes of anger" (3-5). They are aware of "the history of shame" (7) their land has. They know their land is fully plundered and now filled with "echoes of empty lores" (10). Yet they love their land because it is all they have. In the second part of the poem, the persona concentrates on the oppressor and his praise singers and sycophants with whom he instils silence in the land. The emperor "is fooled by remnant-smiles / of sycophants ... and silence" (17-8). Men, women, and children are deprived of the basic things of their lives as well as their visions. Thus,

> Darkness dawns
> bones break
> madness maims. (19-21)

Yet the dictator is continuously "fooled" (23) by his sycophants and praise singers because they themselves are, according to the poet, "spineless fools" (23). While these sycophants are not silent, shouting the praises of the emperor, they are, in fact, silenced because they cannot open their mouths to utter a word against the oppression which they themselves suffer from.[5] In juxtaposing the voices of the masses side by side with the enterprise of the fools, the poet shows that the dictator has done nothing to be praised but to be condemned and it is mere cowardice that has made the praise singers, with such cheapened consciences, glorify the killer; they are afraid of being killed. It is pertinent to note that the persona in Raji's poems of silence has detached himself from the syndrome of silence. He is either against the masses for keeping silent or against the emperor for scaring the masses into silence.

Raji philosophises on the siren and convoys that accompany the dictator wherever he goes in the three poems that follow. In "Siren Sense I" "Siren Sense II" and "Siren Sense III", the poet exposes, satirises, declaims and curses the phenomenon of official escorts to executive leaders. In the first poem, it is one of the escorts who speaks of the wickedness of the siren motorcade. He dishes out a warning to a passer-by who is likely to have a "date / with the dead at heaven's gate" (24-5), or become "maimed / without a fee being named" (26-7). He has earlier warned:

> be gone when you see us
> our naked light above
> koboko clubbing bayonet banning
> when you smell us meandering
> of a mutinous market. (2-7)

In the above lines, the poet tries to capture the senseless speed and violent nature of the convoys – which is indeed the sense of the siren. The gospel they carry is that anyone or anything on the way should be crushed because the oppressor is passing. In the second poem, the persona is no longer one of the escorts, not concerned whether the person standing on the way is killed or not. The persona is an onlooker, drawing attention to the frightening stillness occasioned in public places (such as markets) by the motorcades of the escorts:

> The market stands naked
> to the emptiness of open  roads...
> the highway is wide, wider
> than the astonishment
> in the public eye. (2-6)

And despite the masses' tradition of standing and staring at the almighty road users, the poet calls his "brother man" (7) and tells him that he is a vulnerable victim of the madness of the convoy. To them he is a "fatal ant" (8) or a "lousy dog" (12) or a "carcass" (14) that they will not hesitate to crush on their way. The third poem is the shortest and contains a virulent verbal attack on the leader travelling in the convoy. The persona bursts out with curses on the leader:

> may the wind carry a convoy of curses ...
> may the wind stab your tribe's trumpet
> may your glowworm scream lead to hell
> may the dumb ditch embrace your bones
> may new brooms descend
> on the dirty tempest
> of your ghastly waste. (5-13)

As the last line shows, the poet-persona wishes the leader a fatal accident. He invokes the wind – an elemental force – to destroy the leader. Indeed, in the persona's tone and utterance we see his limitation. He cannot certainly raise a weapon against the leader; hence he invokes nature to deal with the leader. The first and second poems of the trio have given reason for the outburst in the third poem. Raji might have written these poems at the peak of military dictatorship in Nigeria during which siren escorts and convoys were so rampant that any senior military officer could send the air splitting with the blaring of sirens. Public office holders, traditional rulers and self-professed sycophants were also lured by the power of sirens; the result was a chaos of sirens across Nigeria, and there occurred cases of innocent people being maimed or killed by the convoys and escorts, and no one dared to question the act.

In "A Dozen Monologue", Raji presents the kind of dialectics that we see in Niyi Osundare's "Olowo debates Talaka" (*Songs of the Season*, 38). It is the "we" against "them" argument in which "we" stands for the masses, the poor, or in a Marxist parlance, the proletariat, while "them" stands for the elite, the bourgeoisie. In a dozen couplets of contrasting meanings, Raji shows that while the poor do the toiling, the rich do the harvesting. Hence the theme of "monkey the work, baboon the chop" (as in Nigerian local parlance) is projected. While the poor people "mine the coal" (1), the rich people "spend the gold" (2). Connecting this poem to Nigerian political development, Raji is probably thematising the quarrel that has, for some time, existed between the Niger Deltans and northerners in Nigeria during the successive military juntas and the current civilian dispensation. The Niger Deltans complain that their land produces the oil and other things that bring riches to Nigeria, but it is the northerners (who presumably do not have these natural resources) that are perpetually in government and misspend the riches. In a larger context, the haves and the have-nots in the society are on each side of a divide that Raji has depicted in the poem. "A Mass Prayer" is the poet's invocation of God to save his people from the claws of "slippery / beasts" (30-1). Raji hinges man's current sins on the archetypal "Adam curse" (2) and "Eve's / felony" (17-8). The poet takes a supplicatory tone and does, in fact, intercede on behalf of his people so that they should be forgiven "the nightmare / of sinful inheritance" (23-3). The poem that comes after "A Mass Prayer" shows why there is the need for the poet to intercede. Having a title unique from the poems in this collection, "1995", it may have been written to capture one of the pro-democracy or anti-military demonstrations in south-western Nigeria during the reign of the military generals. The first four lines of the poem with the adjective, "another" indicates that the "wailing moments / measured in contralto" (7-8) described in the poem is a recurrent decimal. As usual, the "heckling tyrants" (12) are responsible for the upheavals. The poet continues to reveal some of the major problems that befall the land under those tyrants. He depicts tribalism in the following lines:

> I have seen them all: nations dividing
> like malicious molecules
> a hexagon of hate
> in their ethnic paste. (13-6)

Tribalism, to say the least, is one of the fundamental factors responsible for under-development in Nigeria. The hyperbole "a hexagon of hate" (15) maximises the depth of hatred – and realities on the ground in Nigeria have shown this – that exists among ethnic groups especially when developmental issues are focused. Again, as in "To the brim, to the brim", Raji deploys the symbols of animals to depict man's animalistic attitudes towards fellow man. In doing this, a streak of satire is noticed. When the poet says that cockroaches are "dreaming a union dance / before the feathery fury / of pecking fowls" (18-20), he does not only mean that the fowls are always out to cruelly eat up the cockroaches, but he is also pointing out that it is stupid of the cockroaches to dream of a "union dance" against the fowls.

It is demonstrably clear that Raji's poems here are *confrontational*. They visibly foreground the spirits and utterances of a fighter-persona who is not only bent on telling the truth as it is but also fighting the oppressor-figure seen to have bastardised the land.

**Of Transformative Trope: The Therapeutic Force of Laughter**
In a collection of mostly political poems, which attempt to capture situations that can evoke tears, laughter may seem to have no place. Indeed, where there are tears, laughter may loss its function and would merely assume a hypocritical or cosmetic stance. It is therefore paradoxical that the poet finds bravery in laughter despite the flow of tears in the land. In fact, it is with laughter that he emerges to tackle the gross inadequacies of the authorities. Which is why laughter translates into a remarkable idiom, a trope to combat the discourse of oppression, in Raji's poetic vision. Since "art," according to Chinua Achebe, "is man's constant effort to create for himself a different order of reality from that which is given to him" (quoted in Okolo 14), the poet Raji, in evolving his art, presents an alternative function of laughter as a balm to the rising temperature of his society with the intention of altering the situation not only for himself but also for the ordinary people

in the society. In this premise, Raji's *A Harvest* is, if closely examined, in an intertextual dialogue with Niyi Osundare's *Waiting Laughters* in which the poet Osundare leads us into the multifaceted explorations of laughter by the oppressor and his cohorts and, at the same time, using laughter as a means of "radical evocation of violence and a retributive force against tyranny of all kinds" (Abdu 141-142). Also swinging from optimism to pessimism, Osundare, now and then, laments that

> Our laughter these several seasons is the simper-
> ing sadness of the ox which adores its yoke,
> The toothless guffaw of empty thunders
> In epochs of unnatural drought. (*Waiting Laughters*, 96)

While the two poets commonly invent a plural form, "laughters", defying the felicity of grammar to perhaps capture the contradiction inherent in the basic concept of laughter and its metaphoric diversities, Osundare's fluidity with the metaphor differs from Raji's inelastic focus on the dual essence of the idiom: laughter of survival and laughter of oppression.

"Black Laughter" reveals more of the poet-persona's resistance against the tyrants of his land. Laughter as an engaging metaphor moulds his strength and provides him an almost harmless weapon with which to live his life in the face of hardship. No matter "the morning mist of harmattan" (2) and no matter "the talcum dust of the day" (11), the persona vows to open his mouth wide and laugh "beyond the thrills and threats / of conditioning yoke" (7-8). There are hideously thrilling realities in his land that threaten his life and he is yoked to strictures and restrictions. The poet's laughter, which he needs to survive, is the one that comes out of the pen because he says, "I need just a pen / for my black laughter" (19-20). The adjective, black, seems to indicate that the poet's laughter carries bravery and endurance associated with the struggles of the black people. Black laughter is the writer's social commitment with which he faces those who have made life oppressive to him and his fellow human beings in the land. The second part of the poem contains three questions in three stanzas.

The poet wonders what amount of energy of the black laughter can "drawn the merry tantrums / of mirthful tyrant" (25-6). In other words, how much of his laughter can withstand the irresponsible anger responsible for the indiscriminate maiming and killing by the military dictator of his land. Part three of the poem answers that question. What the poet needs for survival is "a stubborn cyclone of laughter" (30). This is, in fact, his redeemer "from the teasing scalpels of robbing angels / from tendon-tears of boneless pain" (32-3). Scalpels are sharp blades used for tearing human flesh. It represents the various inhuman policies of the dictators used in inflicting avoidable but damaging pains on the common people. The poet's laughter against such wicked people must carry obduracy and fearlessness, two important qualities of the social activists that were able to stand against dictatorship during the heinous regimes of General Babangida and late General Abacha in Nigeria. The poet yearns for "blue wind" (40), a phrase that occurs twice, signifying the dreamt freedom that will also come as "the dimple breath of dawn" (42). In any case, the poet is not too optimistic about this change and hence whether it is "dusk or dawn" (49) he calls on his black laughter to sustain him during such a terrible time.

In "The Last Laugh" Raji comes out once again as a brave poet, courageous enough to show his people the therapy of laughter in the face of tyranny. The poem is in two parts. In the first part, the poet accuses a "you" (1), which stands for the oppressor, of being wicked towards him. The oppressor "laughed and laughed" (1) – not the kind of laughter the poet knows – at the poet-persona and by doing so expects the poet to fall to his "teasing tongue, red with thorns" (5). It is the laughter that consumes the innocent. The poet-persona boasts that he survives that laughter and this surprises the oppressor's "clan of conspirators / who loved to lick [his] bones / to the music of mockery" (7-9). The poet does not only survive, but is poised to counter the oppressor with his own kind of laughter. Thus the second part of the poem, bold in sanguinity, presents the poet as a possessor of laughter that heals the people:

> The poet in me mocks you too
> But I will rather heal your septic sins
> with a deodorant smell of the last laugh
> I'll rather heal your clan
> with the long lacerating blade of divine love. (19-23)

This is Raji's vision as a poet. He sees the poet as someone, like other poets such as J. P. Clark-Bedekeremo, Osundare and Ofeimun have seen, who should be out to speak the "lacerating" (23) truth to save humanity. Raji dwells on laughter as a cushion for his vision and demonstrates that even in the absence of sanity, of love, of hospitality, and of comfort; in the presence of deafening chants from the dictator and his acolytes, it is the poet's kind of laughter that the people need to learn to be able to go through the hard times. The optimism is continued in "Turn", a short and epigrammatic poem. The poet invokes the power of a supernatural being, probably God, to turn darkness to light. His death will thus become "butter-fly melodies of love" (6). His tears will turn to "golden rosary of laughter" (9). The image Raji has created here, hinged on Catholicism – we know of the power that is said to reside in the Rosary – is expected to have a kind of liberating effect on humanity. Just as the rosary saves, so also the laughter that bears what the poet has captured in the metaphor "rosary" is expected to save the poet and his people. This poem is also well positioned because the optimistic view of the poet through the preceding elegies is summarily presented in a strong tone. As in some of his poems, the supernatural being addressed is seen as capable of intervening for the poet and his nation.

The last part of *A Harvest of Laughters* contains only one long poem titled "Harvest I-VI." The poem, more discursive than others, totalises the strands of vision the poet has pursued in the collection. Raji succeeds in elevating laughter to a metaphor that is capable of surmounting the poverty and wants that are responsible for the pitiably low standards of living in the land.

Since the military dictator is responsible for causing that in Raji's poetry, laughter, here, is used as a poetic strategy of combat against the dictator. Hence, the poet Raji, as Okolo puts it, approaches his

> task as [a] social act that entails evaluating the mode of production in society; the nature of the relationship between the various classes; and how to bring about a revolutionary end to the oppression and exploitation by one class of another. (100)

The poet's dream, demonstrated in his poems here, is to bring an end to the lingering social crisis between the rich and the poor; because of this, he deploys various poetic strategies, institutes tropes and evolves a resilient voice. Raji's rhetoric of laughter inheres on the potency of a social art. In "Harvest I-VI", the poet concludes his running theme that "Laughter can heal" (22). It is divided into six parts. In part one, the poet reveals the uncomfortable condition in which people live in the country: "a blind moon bleeds across the streets / a dominion of silken dust sickens this wind" (6-7). It is indeed terrible for the moon, itself a light for humanity, to be blind, talk less of bleeding. That it bleeds shows that some people (the oppressor and his men) have inflicted violence on it. And that it bleeds in the streets shows that all the people are affected by – and thus suffer from – the wound of the moon. The second line carries "silken dust" as a strong metaphor. The dust, despite its silken beauty, moves in the wind and does damage to people's eyes. This is violence on the people. The poet reiterates the bad situation in the second part of the poem. The land is yet filled with "so many stitches so much pain "(8). The poet-persona harks back to the evils perpetrated by the oppressor and his cohorts in the past. He refers to them as "boa-conspirators" (10) because of the terrible way they conspire to oppress the masses. He also refers to them as "pagan pilgrims" (11) all bearing "ribbons of snakes" (12), lustily set to act on the "virgin plague" (13). These metaphors evoke sharp images that depict the wickedness of those who cause others to suffer.

Part three of the poem introduces what the people need to live through the gloomy situation – laughter. The poet tells his people in a clear term that "if only [they] know the crescent magic of Laughter" (16). Laughter is written with capital "L" to show its supra-abstract nature. It is seen as a concrete reality, a formidable substance, capable of setting people free from their poor and harsh conditions. When we know the magic of laughter, then

> we will ride the flood of predicted pains
> we'll toast to a tomorrow full of love
> without stitches or stains
> without brimstones of plagues
> without milestones of snakes. (17-21)

Raji's metaphor of pain and suffering above attests to his deep understanding of the crises-ridden Nigeria he writes about. Ultimately, "snakes" bite and their poison kills. It is to that extent that the destroyers intend to kill the land. Laughter, the poet says in the next lines, can heal the bites of the snakes. But in spite of the capacity of laughter to heal, the poet is not oblivious to the fact that laughter may, sometimes, disappear from man. In part four of the poem, he dwells on the interregnum between one laughter and the other during which it is possible that "dark clouds cripple the cheeks / as dimples vanish into bleak oblivion" (24-5). The image of crippling cheeks, i.e. contorted face, reveals the absence of laughter and the presence of pain. This image demonstrates that Raji has a close understanding of the philosophy of laughter, of the contours of the face when laughter comes upon it, and the crisis of emotion that is capable of chasing laughter away from the human face. The poet turns to the oppressor in part five. He does not hurl invectives on the oppressor as we see in other poems, but offers a curse that sounds like a prayer. He prays that the oppressor should know the difference "between the bloodbath and the birthcry" (36). As simple as this difference seems, it appears the oppressor has forgotten about it and that is why he pursues his cruel acts relentlessly. It is also important for the oppressor to know the difference "between the ash and tinders of joy" (40) and "between the cruel scar [inflicted by him] and tattoos of love" (42). And in this knowledge, laughter's fingers will lift the veil of oppression the oppressor has hidden himself in. When the veil is lifted, the oppressor becomes equal with the people he oppresses. At this level, nemesis is wont to catch up with the oppressor. The last part of the poem presents to us different complexions of laughter, attaching each of them to its functional posture. The first is "a callous laughter / ... / of a blistering sun" (45-7). This may be the oppressor's laughter because of how inhuman it sounds. The next one is "a lean laughter" (48) which is found in "swaying stem" (49), a metaphor whose import is the unsettled man in the discomfort created by the oppressor. The bees' "pollen laughter" (51) is the laughter of production, of sweet and pleasurable moments ahead. The "gentle laughter" (54) is also that of good life. In the stanzas that follow, the poet concentrates on the healing effect of laughter and ultimately points out that, no matter the situation, "Laughter lives / on the verdant breath of Nature's wings" (67-8).

Raji's duty as a poet is to go into the "breath of Nature's wings" and pluck laughter for humanity and he performs the duty quite well. This results in the unusual conferment of transformative power on laughter. As Bakhtin puts it, "[f]ear is the extreme expression of narrow-minded and stupid seriousness, which is defeated by laughter" (47). Raji seeks to offer his nation the kind of laughter that can defeat their state of fear. More than anything, Raji establishes himself in his first collection as a poet with a deep love for humanity, for people around him, and for his land. He does not claim to carry the gospel of the therapy of laughter to the entire world. He is a poet more sensitive to his immediate environment. His later output may prove this wrong, though. In A Harvest, Raji builds a sustainable theme of survival, even in stark situation of penury and oppression, for himself and, above all, for the people of his country ravaged by successive military juntas.

## Notes

1. Here, we refer to the most terrible dictators in Nigerian history, namely, General Ibrahim Badamosi Babangida (1985-1993) and late General Sani Abacha (1993-1998).

2. One of the overwhelming ambitions of the Nigerian dictators General Babangida and General Abacha was to transform themselves from military rulers into civilian leaders. It was widely known as the second coming.

3. See Chimamanda Ngozi Adichie. *Purple Hibiscus*. Lagos: Farafina, 2004.

4. See Wole Soyinka. *The Man Died: Prison Notes*. Ibadan: Spectrum, 1985.

5. The phenomenon of praise singing is entrenched in Nigeria's history of dictatorship. Olusegun Adeniyi brings this to our knowledge when he says, "[f]rom Gowon to Obasanjo, Buhari to Babangida and now Abacha, Nigeria has always been awash with time servers who become willing tools under the military rulers with the idea of self succession" (*The Last 100 Days of Abacha*, 39). Interestingly, Adinyi himself was now a time server for Umaru Yar'Adua's regime, seen by many as an extension of Olusegun Obasanjo's.

# CHAPTER

# 4

A *Harvest of Laughters* creditably announces a poet, with his unusual signature trope, fully persuaded to combat the emperor on behalf of the people in his society. He institutes laughter as his idiom – an idiom that recognises the carnivalesque essence of common people bound by communal desires. He positions himself at the centre of different shades of laughter and makes what we may consider as his first definitive move. Reading his subsequent volumes we have the impression that the first collection is a preamble to his real discourse of political engagement. The harsh tone of the first collection, as visibly orchestrated as it is, gives way to a harsher tone in Raji's second collection of poetry. The images become more piercing. The reason for this, we may surmise, is the closeness of Raji's poetry to the real socio-political happenings in Nigeria. It does appear that the first collection historicises the dictatorship of Gen Ibrahim Badamasi Babangida while the second historicises that of the late Gen Sani Abacha. It is common knowledge that the latter is worse than the former, hence the harsher, more intense tone of *Webs*. We will concentrate on Raji's second volume on this chapter and show Raji's keen poetic eye as a chronicler, a town crier (in the sense Christopher Okigbo uses the term), in his country Nigeria. He continues to pursue his interventionist vision in this volume, focusing particularly on the species of intellectuals, the writers, who suffer most in a junta because of their irrepressible spirits.

**Webs of Remembrance: Realising the Aesthetics of Rage**
Raji's second collection, *Webs*, promises a more solid base to

institute himself as a political poet. It arguably contains his best political poems. Some of the poems are carried over from his first collection because they obviously fit into the poetic vision of this collection and should have been preserved for it. Part of the success of the collection stems from the strength of the imagery the individual poems embody. Raji's images reveal a more enraged, confrontational poet, although in his statement of vision prefacing the collection, Raji says that he is just remembering: "I opt to remember and make others remember" (9). Beyond remembering, Raji does not only confront but he also courageously hits at the military dictators hard with blows of severe images. With a venomous tone, considering the choice of his diction, the poet is apparently out for a total war against the military. Since the poems were written in the heyday of the worst military dictatorship in Nigeria, Raji's poetisation would be seen as a "programme of action" towards paying what Osundare calls the price of freedom. Osundare opines that "[t]he price of freedom is eternal vigilance. We [writers] must be part of that vigilance. We must expose all those things that dictators are always trying to hide" (Interview with Omowunmi, 39). Anyone who wrote under the maximum ruler's dictatorship was certainly paying the price of freedom.

"This land tickles me" presents a persona who is tickled not by playful pleasure or good things but by the evils he remembers. Tickle becomes ironic here. It is supposed to evoke laughter of pleasure but certainly not this one because the pleasure of this tickle is "grilled / in pints of pain" (2-3). The poet narrates the many woes of the land, taking us to the climax of military oppression. The land is "...full of tongues / ... without memories / [w]ithout herbs of a waking sense" (4-6). The military rulers and their men hardly learn from history; mistakes are repeated senselessly. What the poet refers to as the land here are actually the people, the underprivileged, who are at the receiving end. The land is also full of "Naked gods..." (8) who parade themselves as messiahs "On rot and starched rust" (10). They are the kind of men Olusegun Adeniyi refers to as "old brigade" (28). The line describes soldiers who have rotten consciences, whose bravery, the poet says, is on their "tattered stripes" (11). Using the image of a wicked surgeon whose "hand that holds the scalpel is blind" (14), Raji presents, quite pointedly, the mercilessness of the bad leaders in inflicting pains on the people of the land. He paints the criminal activities that seethe the land because new thieves emerge daily (since young men do not have jobs to engage them). The poet concludes that

> This land tickles me so soft, so hard and soft
> I cannot forget its vanity, its melody of stones
> This land tickles me without end ... (21-23)

A people who have nothing other than a "melody of stones" are doomed, denied a future. To taste of good life, there must be a rhythm of life available to the people. This is turned into a stone through the deliberate activities of soldiers who seize power in the land. This poem does not bear the Rajian optimism because the land obviously has unending inclinations and actions to keep tickling the persona. There are no solutions in sight for the problems the poet has presented in the poem. The land's "melody of stones" (23) does not bear – and is not capable of bearing – life for its people either now or in future. So, the poet is resigned to his fate.

"Cyclone I" to "Cyclone IV", are four poems that are sparks of the poet's feeling towards the plunder of the land. "Cyclone I" is worth quoting wholly here:

> Nightmare flickers
> In our twice-thrice-beaten
> Eyes, no more meaning
> In the gram, no gram
> In the grammar of lives
> My pain goes
> Like a stubborn present
> Tense.

The poet evokes nightmarish incidents that beat people's imagination during the military eras in Nigeria. Life becomes meaningless with those incidents. Raji's pun on "gram" and "grammar" attempts to capture the weight of the feeling exerted on the people by the nightmare. The poet speaks of the people's suffering and then narrows it to himself. His pain, "Like a stubborn present / Tense" (7-8), will not leave him, its persistence is killing. The poet, like his fellow country people, becomes a perpetual sufferer. Under this condition, he cannot create. Ola Rotimi states his experience of this police state when he writes, "[an] enduring state of anomie engenders malaise and disenchantment. This state is so unsettling in virtually every respect that it disorients and even frustrates the will to create or to produce" (126). Under this condition, there was an exodus of Nigerian writers and activists to the West in the 1990s.

"Cyclone II" talks of the relief that comes on the heels of the stubborn pain of the previous poem. "A slender relief / Touches Earth's brow" (3-4). Then those who belong to the clan of the oppressors go berserk. Their becoming "restless" (12) and "Speechless..." (13) indicates that indeed people will have some respite from the activities of the evil ones. This did occur in the history of Nigeria when a new military leader took over power and offered temporary relief to the suffering people, only for him to plunge the nation into deeper sorrow.[1] Then, again, "Darkness springs" (1) return in "Cyclone III". The dictator reclaims his evil hands. The people naturally "reap the bounty / Of griefs newly grown" (3-4). In a couple of images Raji presents the battered land with its "harvest of poisons / Sewn in Earth's veins" (9-10). Raji uses sheep as a metaphor for the innocent people who become the "garnished game / Of blood in the wind." (14-5). This represents the indiscriminate killings that are the result of inordinate passion on the part of the evil emperors. "Cyclone IV", characteristic of Raji's poems of hope, consoles us that the wind carrying the game of blood in the previous poem contains evil and good. Rain serves as a metaphor for hope and harvest. The fire of the wind is not a negative fire because it "licks / The whirlwind" (6-7) that brings nightmare to the people. The poem is oxymoronic in feature and captures the confusion that the wind brings although beyond the dreams and nightmare of the wind rain will fall. These four poems are good because they do not, like some of Raji's political poems, over-thematise. They are short and loaded like Uche Nduka's poems.[2] Raji achieves connectivity among the poems which can be seen in the manner he contrasts them.

"The Predator's Prayer" presents the dictator as animalistic in his drive to throw the land into depression. A predator is either an animal that kills other animals or a person who exploits other persons economically. Raji deploys both senses of the word in his creation of the image of the oppressor. The oppressor is thus animalistic having "a canine promise" (11) that paradoxically soothes and destroys the people at the same time. The predator has an insatiable belly into which he pours all that he destroys, and he keeps destroying and pouring in. The poet reminds us here of the amazing greed of Nigerian dictators who kept siphoning public funds without any sense of modesty. In dealing with people, the predator has "learnt to perch on the wings of bloody wishes" (1). He says that his love for the people is "malarial" (3), meaning that it sickens and destroys the people. In the scope of this image, malaria should be seen as an illness that kills and is capable of wiping out a generation. The predator is murderous in nature considering his "bloody wishes" (1), his "crocodile jaw" (6) and his "canine promise" (11). The most explicitly message-laden of Raji's poems on military dictatorship in Nigeria is "Malediction for a Maximum Ruler." In the early part of the poem, the poet celebrates his freedom because he is now free to sing. He will "feel no more nightmares" (6) and thus will sing his "harmless song" (9). The freedom of the poet is no doubt as a result of the extinction of dictatorship, since the poet cannot crow for freedom when the dictator is alive. The reason for his being free to sing his song, itself, is nightmarish. Hence:

But I tried most in vain
to kill this knifing nightmare
...
Not to remember the emperor of scars
who forgot his brains
in a luncheon of prostitutes. (13-18)

The dictator, the maximum ruler, is the "emperor of scars" because
he is adept at inflicting sorrows and scars on his subjects. Lines
17 and 18 above reminds us of General Abacha's misadventure
during which he was said to have lost his life in a sexual orgy
with prostitutes. Karl Maier captures this aspect of Nigerian
history thus: "It began on June 8, 1998, when Abacha, on his
customary nightly excursion into the pleasures of the flesh,
expired while in the arms of a pair of Indian prostitutes. The
official cause of death was a heart attack, although
unsubstantiated rumours abounded concerning his demise" (4).
Indeed the dictator in this poem, variously referred to as "the
beast" (6), "the emperor of scars" (16) and "NEBUCHADNEZZAR"
(44), is easily seen as late General Abacha. It is this dictator that
scared every person in Nigeria "with threats of self-succession"
(24). He is trained "of Amin-Bokassa-Doe-Sese-Seko School" (29).
This alliterative listing of the most feared dictators in Africa shows
the gravity of the dictator's oppression. It also shows that the
Nigerian history of woes is a part of a larger history: Africa has
been wallowing in a trajectory that moves from slavery to
colonialism and to neo-colonialism dramatised in the diverse post-
colonial instabilities on the continent.

The triumphal tone of the poet is realised in stanza four where
he prays that all that is done in worship and apotheosis of the
dictator should "be burnt" (40). That not withstanding,

Let an epitaph of piss be written:

HERE ROTS NEBUCHADNEZZAR FOREVER
KING OF LOOTERS... (44-46)

The poet considers it indeed triumphal that the very dictator who does not allow him to sing his song will now have his epitaph written in piss. An epitaph by the way is expected to say something good about someone dead. This poem is entirely a paradox in which the poet attempts to show – in lucid language – the gravity of an oppressor's cruelty and the eventual collapse of his oppression. The poem summarises the life and death of a dictator whose actions are not only wicked to his subjects but also to himself because he is inept enough to forget "his brain" (17) on the laps of prostitutes.

The venom encased in Raji's diverse images on the person and junta of the late General Abacha speaks volume of the poet's position about the unending plunder of his land since independence. Rage, or livid anger, becomes something of a trope in *Webs*. Like Chiedu Ezeanah's poetry, Raji's versification of the intense military oppression in Nigeria here reveals a tortured soul clawing at the walls of oppression erected by the dictator to establish the disturbing divide between him and those he ruled. Consequently each poem here becomes a substance, and an act: indeed a stone (following "a melody of stone") hurled at the oppressor. The eventual death of the oppressor, even if he does not die of poetry but of heart attack (which was really a perfect way of dying of the sulphuric metaphors Raji and other poets threw at him in the 1990s), only confirms, in a way, the *potency* of the aesthetics of rage raised against the ruler.

**Emperor versus Writer: a Critical Intervention**
Part of the realities of dictatorships Raji aptly captures in his political poems is the oppression of the writer / journalist in Nigeria. Other poets and writers have captured the ugly situation in their works, too.[3] It is common knowledge that during the years of General Muhammadu Buhari, the notorious Decree Two was promulgated to take care of journalists whose confrontational writings, no matter how slight, were taken as seditions. General Ibrahim Badamosi Babangida's junta saw the unprecedented murder by parcel bomb of one of the finest journalists of his

time, Dele Giwa of the *Newswatch* magazine. The dictatorship of late General Sani Abacha was responsible for the judicial murder of Ken Saro-Wiwa, a well-known writer, along with others, despite national and international outcries that the dictator should spare the life of Saro-Wiwa. Maier captures the killing of Saro-Wiwa thus:

> [w]orld outrage against Nigeria reached its peak in November 1995, when the government executed Saro-Wiwa and eight other activists of the Ogoni people in the Niger delta who had campaigned for political autonomy and reparations from Shell for environmental damages caused by its oil operations. Nigeria was suspended from the Commonwealth of former British colonies. (18)

The killing of Saro-Wiwa, let it be pointed out, attracted loud declamation because he was a known figure. There were many unknown persons who were silently murdered while in prisons or killed during demonstrations by the dreaded military regimes.

Writing and publishing suffered immensely in the perilous time of persecution. Under the yoke of tyranny, the educational system collapsed, reading culture became zero. The publishing houses, in the words of Charles Nnolim, "suffered demise" (2). In her introduction to *25 New Nigerian Poets*, one of the very few efforts to publish creative works at the time, Toyin Adewale, explains the collapse of literary production in Nigeria:

> The literary renaissance joyfully announced by Harry Garuba in his introduction to *Voices from the Fringe* [1988]...is today non-existent. The intervening decade between 1988 and now was burdened by the military regimes of General Ibrahim Babangida and General Sanni [sic] Abacha. The decade beheld the betrayal of our political will, the annulment of the June 1993 elections, the murder of human rights and political activists including...Ken Saro Wiwa.... Some young Nigerian writers...chose to go into voluntary exile. Literary groups like the Nigerian Poets League petered out. The publishing

sectors sneered at Nigerian creative literature rejecting it as unprofitable and chose instead to publish school textbooks and self-serving biographies of retired and serving army generals. (iii)

This period of unspeakable depression, a period that, according to Ola Rotimi, "frustrates the will to create" (126), is well dramatised in Maik Nwosu's *Invisible Chapters* (2001) and Helon Habila's *Waiting for an Angel* (2002).

In the poem "My Soul is Stitched," written for Kunle Ajibade, who suffered incarceration under the Abacha regime, the persona comes out fully with an identity.[4] He is a singer, a poet, who defies the pall of silence on the land and breaks "the emperor's / testicles in a nutshell / crash of screaming songs" (1-2). He is no doubt bold, courageous and confrontational. But he pays for it because the emperor and his cohorts "have covered [his] head / with ash, hot as hell" (4-5). Social activists, journalists and writers suffered from the military misrule of the 1990s in Nigeria. Prominent among them was Gani Fawehinmi, who, by 1996, had been detained twenty-seven times (see, for instance, Akpuda 48). This poem treats this issue successfully. The persona laments that he is violently treated because he goes about his duty of checking social ills through his art. He does not only break the emperor's "testicles" (2) – a strong metaphor from Raji's repertoire – he also "rode in a paddle / of proverbs against the aching / currents of an envious sea" (6-8). More than that, he

... caught our drunken gods
in a beastly pose
and sold the canvas
to sneering mortals. (11-5)

This is what writers and journalists do no matter how hostile the dictator is. It is part of their chosen duty to expose the evils of the oppressor as Raji has done in his poetry. The "drunken gods" (11) move in "envious sea" (8) and unleash untold hardship on the people. The persona has a daring gut and, despite what he suffers, is optimistic that "they cannot kill the truth" (19) of his songs and his writings. This fearless optimism reminds one of the Lagos print media that compelled General Babangida to *step aside* in 1993; that consistently deafened late General Abacha's ears till he died in 1998. Kunle Ajibade, himself a victim of undue abuse and harassment, writes of his resolution, along with other founding editors of *TheNews*, one of the magazines under the heavy hammer of the dictator: "[we] resolved to fight to the very end. It was one of those moments when we were not sure we would win, but we were just sufficiently motivated by ideals, which we thought would make our country outlast hopelessness" (5). At the end their persistence and perseverance in the interest of the nation paid off.

"An Underground Poem" is dedicated to Jack Mapanje, probably written in the early 1990s when Mapanje suffered repeated incarcerations from his nation's authorities. In it we encounter the brave persona again; he claims that he cannot be killed even though he has dared to "speak against gods" (14). Already he says "My body is a temple / of angry music" (1-2) which of course must be sung no matter whose ox is gored. Being the only survivor where "melodies are made / on platters of skull" (7-8), he sees himself as capable of laughing at the dictator who is only big by the size of his evil and can do nothing to help the land despite his messianic message. Fearlessly he dares to go on speaking

> Against gods whose flesh refuse
> to melt or dance
> to fires of simple songs
> all of me is a household of canine bravery. (27-30)

Raji carries his optimism in the stubborn, resilient voice of his persona, symbolic of his belief that only the people, when hardened and resistant, can save themselves from the claws of bad leadership.

"Sesan Ajayi, 1959-1994" (in *A Harvest*), written for the writer late Sesan Ajayi is a different kind of elegy. The persona of the poem is seen as someone who understands that death is inevitable, although one ought to accomplish something before one dies. The first couplet presents the poet that should be accomplished before he dies. If the poet does not accomplish his enterprise of singing and laughing before his death, then he should be stirred out of the depth of "Nothing" (13) where death will take him. There, his skill will be useless. This poem regrets that late Ajayi did not live to sing his song to the end. But he did sing a song when he was alive. He was one of those poets, under the tutelage of the Ibadan-based Poetry Club, who wrote out of anger against the military dictator of the day.

"Deadlines" (in *A Harvest*) is written for Dele Giwa, Ken Saro-Wiwa, Mamman Vatsa and others. They were said to have lost their lives to the cruelty of the dictators during the military era in Nigeria of the 1980s and the 1990s, the period well historicised in Raji's corpus and the entire writings of his generation. The poet addresses the oppressor in the poem, reminding him of how he has caused "a mascara of mourning in the land" (2); of how he has fed his "beast / with the flesh of suckling birds" (3-4); of how he has filled his "tongue / with darts of denials and lies" (5-6); and of how he has "killed laughter / like a cruel coward" (6-7). The metaphor "suckling birds" stands for the great potentials that are embedded in the young writers. Killing them means destroying the future as far as creative writing and journalism are concerned. That is how the poet and others see the cruel extermination of Dele Giwa and Ken Saro-Wiwa in the heydays of their productivity. In the second part of the poem, the persona now becomes the land that owns the murdered talents. The same killers have turned to console her. But she points out that it is meaningless because "how do you console a mother / bereaved by the talons of a tiger?" (16-7). This calls to mind some of the programmes that subsequent governments have put up to console the relations of those killed undeservedly.[5] The poet's opinion is that such consolation is useless. Raji continues his exposure of the bad leaders and their destructive misrule and oppression against writers in "Notes of an Exiled Poet" (in *Webs*). He speaks from the view of an exile, although, earlier on, we see a poet-persona resisting the tempting – and often legitimate – idea of going on exile. Raji uses anthem, Nigeria's national anthem, a song of unity and progress, as a metaphor of rot. In stanza one the anthem is empty, only filled with fools who cannot certainly repair the land. In the second stanza, there is the image of a "suicide hole" (7) on the anthem, indicating self-destruction. It is Nigerians that are engaged in plundering Nigeria. No one can salvage the country. This is what the poet means when he says:

> no surgeon can see
> no healer can stitch when Death reaps
> and the roads become desolate
> under her scythe of darkness. (9-12)

Raji's image of "the scythe of darkness" is among his very sharp and incisive images that reveal his deep sense of appropriate imagery. The darkness eclipses people to death. The anthem has "requiem" (13) and "only Truth can heal" (14). The land is barren of truth, a national truth, needed for the development of the nation and humanity. Because this truth is non-existent, "heroes [are] hounded like villains / and thieving necks / now wear garlands of gold" (16-8). It is a society in which people use riches to acquire anything under the sun, including dignity! Such is the tragedy of the land. The poet refers to the melody of the anthem as "terrible" (19). Thus owls feast on the melody and the poet sees "A dead slow march of laughters" (24). This is pessimistic indeed. But the last stanza brings up the optimism:

> I shall come to chorus when I see the end
> of my land's strangled sighs and no more
> the piercing cries behind the bars. (29-31)

The cries will surely end. And the anthem shall be purified anew where oppressors shall have no opportunity to hijack it from the lips of the people for and about whom the anthem is made and sung.

Another successful poem with this theme is "And the Poet Foresees a Death" (in *Webs*) which carries a strong image of "the green tree" (1) burning while every creature "holds their breath in ruins of smoke" (2). Green trees are not meant to burn but flourish. It is a sign of immeasurable havoc that a green tree is burning. Tantamount to the sun setting at noon, Raji's insight into the destruction caused by the past military rulers is quite deep. When the military rulers came, drumming their messianic intents of saving the country from her myriad of problems, one thought they were serious about that. But they turned out to be the worst leaders and set the green tree, a symbol of a flourishing nation at its robust stage, burning to the extent that:

> Restless hills, bleeding woods
> Wounded valleys without echoes of flowers
> Ceremonies in the wind; all else
> Hold their breath in streams of smoke. (10-13)

The weaverbirds and the river-birds, metaphors for singers and poets, are disturbed; they become unproductive. Then the "dove absconds / With her secret of peace" (8-9), giving way to violence. Green trees symbolise the natural resources, the formidable cream of the society, the thinkers and philosophers who are supposed to move the nation forward but cannot because the military ruler plunders and kills and sends them away. We see more of this in "A Country Writes Her Own Epitaph" (in *Webs*), dedicated to Ogaga Ifowodo and Akin Adesokan, two writers who are Raji's contemporaries. They also suffered incarceration during the heinous regime of late General Sani Abacha. The persona of this poem is the Nigerian nation (paradoxically writing her own epitaph). As a plundered, raped mother, she recounts the many woes that have befallen her. The totality of her woes is captured in these lines:

> From the beginning of night
> To the end of day
> Vigils for death become the new

dance-craze of my people. (1-4)

The ultimate is death and it holds sway over the land. Raji's hyperbole is understood here to mean the incessant killings that filled the military juntas that humbled the Nigerian state. As a result the country laments that "My children flee to other lands / Seeking the kindness of strangers" (17-18). The poet points out in the following stanza that the children have to run away because they are "Afraid of the noose and the acid" (26), an image that reminds us of how the writer and environmentalist Ken Saro-Wiwa was killed during the height of the Abacha dictatorship.[6] There is a deep sense of pessimism and loss as the country, a mother, continues her cry because "no one, not even the dead / Is safe / From these vigils / Of a new destruction" (37-40) brought upon the land by the oppressor. Raji abandons his optimism here in a bid to bring before us the gritty realities of violence against the populace and the writers during the military despotism that ruined Nigeria.

Raji's historicism is vivid and engages our memories with pictures of the suppression of journalists and writers in an age in which the land is barren of democracy. In spite of the pessimistic tone of some of the poem, there is a theme of irrepressibility running through all the poems; the writers/journalists will simply not give up in the face of tyranny. Raji's poems here, apart from posing as acts of intervention, celebrate the bravery of this select class of people who under the terrible regimes of the 1980s and the 1990s in Nigeria took extra-ordinary measures, such as guerrilla journalism and chapbook and self-sponsored publishing, to confront the cruel authorities of the day.

**Notes**

1.  A good example is the case of General Babangida. When he took over power in 1985, Nigerians were tired of the oppressive blows of General Mohammadu Buhari one of which was the notorious Decree Two that hounded journalists and sent them into prison without trials. When General Babangida came,

he struck it out and endeared himself to Nigerians. But, alas, it was during his regime that journalism received the harshest blow: the killing by parcel bomb of Dele Giwa, one of the finest journalists in Nigeria then.

2. See, for instance, Uche Nduka. *If Only the Night*. Amsterdam: Sojourner Press, 2002.

3. See, for example, Chimamanda Ngozi Adichie's first novel, *Purple Hibiscus* (2004), and Sefi Atta's first novel, *Everything Good Will Come* (2005).

4. Kunle Ajibade was one of the journalists who suffered severe incarceration during the intense dictatorship of General Sani Abacha. He was sentenced to life imprisonment but was set free when General Abacha died. He produced a prison memoir titled *Jailed for Life*.

5. In most cases, the government decided to train the children of the slain talents or offer their wives jobs as a form of compensation for the death of their breadwinner.

6. It was common knowledge that when Ken Saro-Wiwa was hanged in 1995, acid was poured on his body in order to be sure that it was totally destroyed. The dictator had a special interest in ensuring that nobody had access to the body of the slain writer.

# CHAPTER

# 5

In *A Harvest* and *Webs*, Remi Raji primarily concerns himself with raising a voice, coherent and confrontational, against the hegemonic power of the military in a post-independence Nigeria. Beneath that is of course his interventionist voice that stridently decries the undue subjugation of not only the generality of the people but also special classes of people such as creative writers and journalists. The question of oppression and the fate of the people under tyranny is also, inevitably, his concern in his third volume *Lovesong*, a volume in which, following Odia Ofeimun, he marries choreography and poetry with a considerable degree of dramaturgy. Aside from the form, this volume differs from the earlier ones in that it is more evocative of the poet's nation, Nigeria; indeed it traces the history of Nigeria (her plunder, her brutalised people, her resilience in remaining as a nation) and reads like a tribute to Nigeria on the occasion of its forty-five years of existence as a sovereign state. In this chapter, our attention will be focused on Raji's negotiated move, in consonance with his historicism, from the images of plunder through the images of reconstruction to the images of a reclaimed, better future for his country.

### *Lovesong for My Wasteland*: Nation, Voice, Vision
Raji takes a significant step, higher, as a nationalist poet, in his fourth collection. He moves beyond the engagement of abusive attacks on depraved leaders, lamentation for deprived and dehumanised masses, to a more holistically coherent nationalist voice that presents, to us, a poet, like Aime Cessaire, who "does

not only sing Martinique, [but] is Martinique" (Moor 153). Raji is Nigeria in *Lovesong*. Each sequence of the long-breath poem carries the spirit of Nigeria in a flow of images that pull to picture Nigeria's tattered past, confused present and an envisaged optimistic future. Raji surprisingly finds influence in one of the most influential writers of the twentieth century European literature, T. S. Eliot. Raji's title, "Lovesong for my Wasteland" loudly echoes Eliot's two famous, well-discussed poems: "Lovesong of Alfred J. Prufrock" and "The Waste Land". He quotes lines from the former to open this volume of poetry:

> For I have known them all already, known them all-
> Have known the evenings, mornings, afternoons,
> I have measured out my life with coffee spoons;
> I know the voices dying with a dying fall
> Beneath the music from a farther room.
> So how should I presume? (*Lovesong for My Wasteland,* 1)

Raji, here, cashes in on the all-knowing image to stamp his understanding of the pains and joys of his land. Asked if by drawing an influence from Eliot he is not incurring the Chinweizuan brand of criticism that forbids African writers to be Euro-centric, Raji explains,

> No, a Chinweizu or the version of the combative anti-Enlightenment critic of African poetry does not worry me. I think we make so much out of the echoes of Eliot in the title, [but] beyond that you will rarely find the usual Anglo-American opaqueness of style that a Chinweizu will kick against in the text itself.... I think there is no better canonical way to symbolise the imagination of my land in the metaphors already internationalised by Eliot. If I deploy the tropes of "love" and "wasteland" for a distinctive constructive purpose, if I domesticate them and the reader is touched differently by the power of the metaphors and the message, why worry then? (*In Their Voices and Visions,* 86)

The title, whether its echoing Eliot is a point of worry or not, aptly underscores the nostalgic, elegiac tone and tenor that are engagingly coherent throughout the volume.

This volume is differentiated from Raji's other volumes by the poet's patronage of agrarian imagery. The first sequence (which I will also call verse in this work), "IN THE BEGINNING OF A SEASON" (this capital and subsequent ones are the poet's) asks an important question that preoccupies a farmer in the beginning of a season. A farmer should, ordinarily, think of "when to sleep, how to harvest or what to plant" (3). But this singer is a farmer with a different preoccupation. He is burdened with a seed for sorrow and trouble for the land. *"This is the seed which grows in my mind / A cancerous tuber nobody wants to eat"* (these Italics and subsequent ones are his, 10-1). The import of this agricultural image is that the singer, this talebearer, has a story that has grown in his mind but nobody wants to listen to it. He however tells the story; people have to listen to it. He begins by saying, "THERE'S A LAND / where the river runs with thirst" (12-3). After pointing out the tension in the land occasioned by intrigues, hatred, anger and imperfection, he parallels the earlier expression with "There's a land / where thirst runs through the river" (19-20). Raji's image of a river here is as limpid as other images in the volume. It is not just the oxymoronic nature of conjoining river and thirst, but the depth of havoc discernible in the image. It shares a thematic direction with the image of the burning green tree that we earlier encountered in *Webs* (see chapter four). Thirst running through the river is an apt image depicting the poverty in the midst of plenty that has been characteristic of a military-ravaged Nigeria, the poet's wasteland. Indeed this syndrome of poverty in the midst of plenty runs throughout Africa, for, as Kofi Anyidoho reminds us, "[this] is the Africa of the intellectual and creative writer's hope and despair, the Africa of the glory of vanished civilizations and of the pain of mass populations set adrift in a world falling apart and yet full of possibilities" (1). This is the Africa that Raji ponders on throughout his *Lovesong*.

In the second verse, the singer-poet indicts everyone of being guilty of wasting the land. "NO ONE IS CLEAN" (1). More so, no one can claim he is free from the consequences of the destruction. This is why "everyone is talking about a cleansing" (6). The singer-poet points out, in the next verse, that people are only pretending; something is indeed wrong with the land. There is "BLEMISH OF HOLES / in that national dress" (1-2). People cover their hunger and anger beneath "fake laughter" (4). The singer-persona is aware of them all. "FORTY FULL SEASONS GONE LIKE YESTERDAY" reveals the stupidity of a nation (indeed of its leaders) which has refused to grow beyond its infant stage. The nation is thus like the "old manchild" (63), one of the pictures of oddities Aboliga the Frog showed his friends in Ayi Kwei Armah's *The Beautyful Ones Are not Yet Born*. The image is that of retardation and dwarfism. According to the poet, even the elders of the land who are supposed to lead the nation forward have lost their legs, their focus. All is stagnant. Imagine the waste of "Two scores and ...seasons gone like yesterday" (8). Very apt about this is Maier's projection that

[s]ince winning independence from Britain in 1960, Nigeria has witnessed at least one million deaths in Africa's biggest civil war, the assassination of two government leaders, six successful coups and four failed ones, and thirty years of army rule. Yet somehow the country has stayed together, despite decades of government by a clique of military and civilian elite who have behaved like...pirates in power. (xxi)

The singer-persona hits the nail on the head by saying that it is the people of the land that are responsible for the stagnancy and maladies all around them. The people simply do not have a direction and hence cannot expect production. They are lazy and misuse their opportunities. They cannot exploit their resources for growth and development. So, they abandon their iron ore, ignore the rain and "kill [their] suns with hurtful glee" (4). These are direct effects of military dictatorship. The singer goes on to say:

> The earth swoons in the farmer's hand
> But all we do is rape the land
> All we know is maim the mind
> All we plant are epitaphs for the dead. (5-8)

These lines are heavy with the images of destruction. The land is not only raped, deprived of its virgin natural resources, the best minds in the land are also maimed. The intellectuals in our midst fled into self-exile during the years of the locusts in Nigeria. And those who dared to remain were often unlucky to be murdered. History records these incidents to lash the singer into singing.

The second part of the volume, introduced by a quotation from Ai Qing's "I love this land", begins with the eleventh verse, "TEN MONARCHS, TEN SEASONS." The word "monarchs" stands for undemocratic governments, coming after one another, responsible for the bastardisation of the singer-persona's land. He tells of the power that restricts human freedom and progress as a result of which "the crossroads are multiplying daily" (3). Silence is one of such. One is either silent or he is silenced because "It is the season of gods. It is the season of dogs" (5). Raji's bringing together of "dogs" and "gods", beyond the assonantal effect, speaks volume of the dog-like greed and animalistic indignity of the nation's leaders who enjoy being self-made gods. As their subjects, one would have to resort to silence or adopt the craft of telling lies. The poet goes on in verse thirteen to talk of aborted dreams. They melt "like shea-butter nut of nothingness in the sun "(2). The paradox of having thirst in the "land of rivers" (3) represents the suffocating poverty in which people live in the midst of plenty in the land. To add to that, the so-called heroes of the land, those people they have come to value and idolise are people whose thoughts are not even deep, whose philosophies cannot give integrity to the land. All these make the persona "borrow laughter from the wind of wonder" (5). And then he becomes a new personality whose "voice captures the loudness of thunder" (8), whose tongue "seeks the magnificence of tender metaphors" (9), and whose ultimate aim is to see to the "end of hardness and pain in the softness of things" (10). This is a duty that he is not just hopping into; it is a long thought out, self-given duty. Raji here gives a portrait of himself as a poet whose works "can set an ideal standard for society and the state" (Okolo 1).

The poet continues to expatiate on the problem of the land in verse seventeen. The inability of the people to use their minds, to engage in constructive thinking and have a deep sense of history has, as Raji has shown from the beginning of this volume, been the cause of the wasteland. The singer-persona laments that "We have long sought the shadow of the masquerader / And we puke in pride and laziness" (3-4). His people are given to pleasure and celebration of mediocrity because of the kind of leadership they have. He reveals the pitiable nature of the land for being so endowed with natural resources and yet begging "the world to feed [her] greed" (7). In such a situation, where is the strength and pride of the country, Nigeria, the so-called giant of Africa? The last stanza of this verse is provocative:

> For those who snore in the glory of self-contentment
> *The past is,*
> *the present is not,*
> *the future is nothing.* (10-13)

The height of irresponsibility from the leaders of a country like Nigeria is their craving for indulging in pleasure from ill-acquired wealth. As they eat they do not think of the future. The future becomes undefined. In the next verse, with a style that makes it different from other verses, the singer-persona reminds us that what was responsible for causing havoc in the past is still there. The metaphors here come out sharp and biting. Having referred to the failure of the past as "CLOUDS", he goes on to liken them to

> the scrotal
> burden
> of
> convicted
> rapists. (8-12)

This image is significant because it brings to our minds the nature of the destroyers who defile the land the way a rapist defiles a woman. The image following it is also sharp: "the smell / in the air / is / the semen / of thieves" (14-9). Raji succeeds in creating an aura of thievery with those lines. This verse is one of the most successful verses in this volume because the imagery we encounter here is able to arouse our anger towards the plunderers in the way that people's anger would be aroused towards a merciless rapist

Raji is not yet done with equating bad leaders with pain-inflicting wild animals as is shown in verse nineteen. He sees the oppressors, the destroyers as "SCORPION" (1), as "crabs" (2) and as "alligators" (3). These animals manifested in the personalities of the oppressors, are "still in greed / for blood and brains of children...." (3-4). Children are the future of the land and once they are destroyed the land loses its future. The past leaders have left nothing useful behind for the people of today. The singer-persona's lamentation here is deep-felt since the land is left with nothing that can be productive as the rivers, a source of eating and drinking, a source of wealth for the land, is already poisoned by no other persons than the owners of the land themselves. Raji dwells on the violence that has become an integral part of the history of the land. The singer-persona considers himself and his generation as "CHILDREN OF THE GUN" (1). Gun metaphorically refers to the militarisation of the Nigerian polity by successive military dictators that held sway over the land for a long time, causing untold damage. They are also "Children of wrath / Ever abandoned to the odour of shame" (2-3). Bayonets and bombs that signify military might with their unique ways of causing deaths are clearly depicted. Consequently, the singer-persona says, "We learn new ways of dying" (6). The culture of violence in the land is also pictured in the people's propensity to brew "wine... / of arsenic, ammonia and hemlock" (7-8) for themselves. They pollute the very air they breathe and are thus responsible for causing their own deaths. Violence, as the singer-persona shows in these lines, is inherent in the people because of their past: "We who munch violence like water-yams / What certainties now lie before us" (11-2)? It is still the lamentation about the reckless past that has failed to create a good future. Foresight and wisdom elude a generation born into the philosophy of oppressive violence. The theme of violence is continued in the next verse. The singer-persona reveals that people have become cannibalistic and feed on the flesh of their fellow people. Using the pronoun "we" consistently because he knows the generation that has begotten him, he says, "We fed on our neighbours' entrails" (2). A sore is created; it expands and becomes part of the life of the people. Raji's portrayal of cannibalism here is identical to Christopher Okigbo's depiction in "Path of Thunder". It is still the same society where life is a game of survival, with the instinct for violence surfacing:

> the elephant ravages the jungle
> the jungle is peopled by snakes
> the snake says to the squirrel
> I will swallow you
> the mongoose says to the snake
> I will mangle you
> the elephant says to the mongoose
> I will strangle you. ("Elegy for Slit-drum", 43-50)

It is the game of the powerful ones preying on the weak ones; it is far from being an egalitarian society.

Verse twenty-two is a strong one that echoes the biblical picture of the end of things and lives. The end time, it is said, is a hard time. It is the age of various criminal and inhuman activities. The end time is the age in which the sinner and the saint can hardly be differentiated from each other because the bad people who will multiply geometrically will take over the affairs of the land. It is the time "When the king is the chief of crooks / And the rapist is next of kin to the therapists" (4-5). It will indeed be the end of things when the thieves can use the law against the innocent people and the assassins will move gently, unknown, as priests in the society. Such time is the time that the society loses its values and the people surrender their lives to God knowing fully that their situation has gone beyond human contrivance.

Although Raji in these poems still identifies the oppressor and his cohorts, calls them by no other names, reduces their human status with animal images, he is more concerned about the battered nation: what is of primary concern here is to rescue the nation from years of repression. The tone is overtly nationalistic. The poet speaks of nation; he also speaks of love. The volume dextrously displays a level of inter-textuality, prefacing its sections with quotes from world renowned poets, such as Ai Qing, Pablo Neruda, and T. S. Eliot, who were in their disparate times and tones concerned about the fates of their nations.

**Town Crier's Poetics: People, Nation, and Optimism**
Raji is aware that the optimism he offers will be useless if the people do not change their habit and attitude towards the oppressors and towards the rehabilitation of their land. Consequently, in some of his political poems, he takes the position of a town crier and dishes out pieces of advice to the people in this respect. His contention is that unless the masses realise their folly, especially in dancing like cowards to the tune of those who seize power to suppress and oppress them, they can never successfully extricate themselves from the grip of military despotism. Such contention is hinged on the functional role of literature in Africa which enables the writer to engage in a useful dialogue with his audience. In his book, *Reading Poetry as Dialogue*, Kimani Njogu posits that

> [the] artist creates from a socio-historical milieu of which he or she is a product and, similarly, the addressee is a social product also informed by the socio-historical events with which he or she is in contact. The literary piece, in turn, reshapes the history of the place and time in which it is received. (10)

Such is the phenomenological basis for the dialogue that goes on between the writer and his audience, whether targeted or not. Raji engages, almost compels, his country people into a dialogue of reconstruction, insisting that they know the nation as much as he does; they share the same history, the same destiny.

In *Lovesong*, after tracing the painful history of plunder, the poet consistently urges the people to drop their old habit of being lackadaisical about the affairs of their land and take active interest in their land since it is the only land they have. For him there is no question of splitting up Nigeria along the lines of ethnicities. He, in the fourteenth verse, calls on those who will join him in emancipating the land to desist from the idea of trivialising the duty. He instructs, "LET THOSE WHO WOULD FOLLOW / Forget the sense of an ending, we have not started" (1-2). It is also pertinent that they should not entertain any fear of falling down, because they have started and all they need is to be on a sound footing. He accuses the people of not being aware of current realities since they live "Ten decades behind the present" (6). They must come to know the present before they can be fully engaged in the duty of shaping a suitable future. Which is why in verse fifteen, he admonishes his country people:

STEP INTO YOUR NEW SELVES WITH NEW HEARTS
Embrace the ground beneath like a virgin bride. (1-2)

The duty calls for people who have understood themselves and have possessed new hearts. This sounds like the biblical baptism that renews and empowers a person to face greater spiritual challenges. The humility and submissiveness of the virgin bride is also needed for successful pursuance of this self-given goal.

The singer-persona continues his admonition to his country people in verse sixteen. The encouragement this time is for the people to "FORGET THE SLOW FACE OF SLOTH AND SORROW" (1). The past should be left behind and whatever pains emanating from the destruction of the past should not stand as a wedge to the progress of this song that also has the phenomenal duty of shaping the future. *"Prime tomorrow with the colour of work"* (2), he admonishes. Without hard work needed to rebuild the destroyed nation, the future may not take shape. Raji's image of destruction in this verse is seen in *"bazaar of bastard"* (3), capturing the kind of unrestricted greed and glee with which the past leaders feasted on the resources of the nation, almost appropriating them to their personal uses. The singer-persona's advice to this generation is that people *"must grow new hearts of steel / And maybe a new definition of love..."* (6-7). Love, now a motif replacing the Rajian laughter, is what this generation needs to advance the rebuilding of a terribly destroyed land. In this shift of idiom, Raji stands out as a poet who is "the sensitive part of his society" (Ojaide, *Poetic Imagination* 35).

"BUT I HAVE LEARNT THE REWARD OF PATIENCE" (1), a line beginning verse thirty-one, replaces the memories of havoc with that Raji's belief in a tomorrow. "My refuge is in songs / laced with the laughter of blades" (2-3). The image created here brings out the confrontational nature of the poet; yet he does not subscribe to making *"melodies with bullets"* (4), which means the demonstrations and upheavals that will amount to insurrections. In other words, he calls for a non-violent action; or, rather, the Gandhian dialectical resistance based on self-respect and self-discipline (see, for instance, Okolo 50-53). It is the patience that allows the human spirits to gather against injustice and move for peaceful cleansing that he needs. He is concerned about the kind of resistance that builds within a man and creates reasonable logic and conviction in the man as to his standing against the evil in the society. Raji's gospel here is that fighting for freedom should be philosophical enough so as not to evoke senseless fighting and destruction. In this verse, Raji reverses Soyinka's lamentation that his generation is a wasted one when he points out that "No more the wasted generation / We must seize the day and wring the neck of night" (8-9). Only the inhabitants of the land can redefine and redirect their future. It is only by themselves they can craft "the story of new loves, new lives, and a new World" (12) which are certainly essential for the progress of the nation.

The singer-poet again concentrates on the oppressor in verse thirty-two. Here, the dictator speaks of the kind of destructive love he has for the land and his modus operandi in plundering the land. He is not given to patience. Haste and greed are in fact what make him a dictator who oppresses people. His love for the land is "malarial" (3) and he thrives on the people's blood. He possesses a "crocodile pouch" (6), a symbol of destructive consumption, and he makes sure that it is always filled with what he can wangle from the people, be it their flesh or their blood. He goes on:

> I asked the gods to take my sight and sharpen my teeth
> That I may descend and rob the earth in my canine
> Softness. (7-8)

In all his endeavours, he is out to make sure that the land surrenders to his expansive wickedness. Raji writes of the dictator's tactics as those of "the colonial angel" (10) capturing the wit and the clever exploits of the African colonial leaders. It is with that kind of passion that the dictator wants to possess the land. Needless to say, the militarisation of the system is a continuation of colonisation, the difference being that the former has home-based actors. The singer-persona goes on, in verse thirty-three, to present himself as a figure of optimism. "But it's about myself in you that I speak / Black, Male, Female, Child, preferably African" (3-5). Already, he is an incurable optimist and he desires that he be seen in his fellow African people. He resists what he terms "the leisure of lazy interpretation" (8) which, at worst, elicits dismal predictions on the land. Despite the past havoc and today's difficulties, the singer-persona's desire is that his "generation shall begin a new correspondence with itself" (13). He calls for a concerted effort to revive the land in its African mirthful essence and recreate the warmth of brotherhood. When this is done, those who think there is no tomorrow for the land will be disappointed. In the last verse in this section, the singer-persona is set to move ahead from the havoc of yesterday and the reality of the movement as "the ready feet of Dawn" (6) calls him for a new and constructive future. He calls on his people, the inhabitants of the land, to come and create "the bedrock of waking in this river of thirst" (8). Out of the river that runs with thirst they must step so as to find their feet in the forward march to a new future. Raji's motif of song surfaces here. The people have to forget the past, put destruction behind them and move ahead as they "*Invoke the humour of the wise...*" (12). This is Raji's gospel of a new Nigeria. It is his way of offering a new metaphor for his nation's self-definition and self-renewal.

Verse thirty-five centres on those who ought to lead the society out of chaos but fail to dream dreams for the land. "AND THE FATHERS OF SECRETS CAST A SPELL / Into future's eyes. All they see is Deceit, sister of Lies" (1-2). They do not have a vision because they have missed the mission they ought to have pursued. The remaining lines of this verse point out the laziness and apparent sense of loss that the people have. It is when they feel hungry that they "talk of rains long imagined" (4). And "the king's men" (7), acolytes of the oppressor, are always there to "mumble an abundance of promise / When famished children howl through empty nights" (7-8). Yet the singer-persona pursues his optimism. Their lack of belief in tomorrow only amuses him. He takes his position, which is different from theirs, because he sees himself as the oracle of the society. And in the next verse, he reiterates his determination to pursue his goal alone:

ALL
all alone
I make my journeys
in tune with a multitude of winds. (1-4)

No doubt he has seen and known of the "indelible marks of rogues" (5), an image that shows the extent to which his land is plundered. He knows quite well how the land is dispossessed. He is, however, determined to face the business of rebuilding it, even if alone. It is a task that he has chosen for himself. To those who are too lazy to follow the noble course he has chosen, he tells the truth in the verse that follows. They are living in "the forge of tears" (2), not ready to come out and emancipate the land. He puts forward a significant proverb for them whose import is that except they build, they do not have a place to live in, and they cannot reap what they have not sown: "The child who gathers imaginary steaks and snails / Will have his supper in a dream of suspended meat" (3-4). Raji's anger and frustration, as a poet, is not only directed towards those who dispossess the land, but also against those who are suffering from the consequences of the dispossession and do not have the courage and will-power to react appropriately. His anger towards the impotent ones comes out clearer in the next verse:

> In the middle of a season
> what should the farmer [do] in the absence of rain:
> burn the wilting seed,
> irrigate the mind of Earth or
> snore away in the compost of despair? (12-6)

Raji's rhetorical question here is aimed at calling and challenging his fellow countrymen into the actions of rebuilding the land. In the previous lines, the singer-persona laments "the smell of bandits" (9) who rule the air. The people of the land should, however, not lapse into despondency but rise and take their future in their own hands.

The last verse in this section, quite elaborate, is a build-up on the previous verse. The singer-persona still indicts his fellow inhabitants of the land for worsening their situation instead of remedying it. Obviously, Raji attempts to capture the disillusionment of the post-military era during which – and it lingers till today – major ethnic groups in Nigeria, instead of building the nation out of the havoc of the military era, became embittered and formed associations and groups with the aim of seeking for redress as each of them was convinced it was marginalised. The deliberate and, often, senseless dirges about marginalisation have not finished yet. Today the government is saddled with the movement for the creation of the sovereign state of Biafra and the movement for the creation of the sovereign state of the Niger Delta.[1] Raji's position is that Nigerians must learn to live beyond this collapse of national psyche. The singer-persona vehemently takes the stand that "I won't, I can't dance in this arena of slit souls / Where they whisper war into empty bowls" (9-10). Even if the dusk is dying, even if the sun (a symbol of vivacity) is sinking, the singer-persona and his children, those he has sold his gospel to successfully, will "embrace the land like a new love" (19). Here is a poet whose nationalist imagination is hinged on what Tanure Ojaide calls the "love of one's country [which] gives rise to ... political poems" (*Winging Words*, 97).

It is with a quotation from Pablo Neruda's "Here I Love You" that Raji opens the last section of *Lovesong*. In a way, Raji's explicit romance with his land essentialised in his political poems here is comparable to Neruda's love poems written for his land. The tones of Raji's verses here are triumphal. The singer-persona has a sense of fulfilment for having given back to his land the hope it has lost, for reviving for the land the future it has almost killed. Raji continues to deploy agrarian images; the images here are quite blended and engaging. The singer-persona is essentially a farmer who believes in the natural law of sowing and reaping. So far, he has been preparing his land, his soil, with the song of remembrance and hope, trying to build a future out of the wreckage of yesterday. In fact, the entire project of versifying the pains and joys of the land, re-contextualising them in a lucid imagistic realm, designing a programme of action for a new nationalism, amount to toiling in the farm. Now, with a sigh of relief, he says:

> I HAVE BUILT MY TENT
> with straws of supple thoughts
> I have watered my farm
> with sweats of longer days...(1-4)

When a farmer, a husbandman, is so prepared, the season will not take him by surprise. His actions will have a direction and rewards will follow them. He positively foresees the fruits of his labour. Having prepared his home and his soil, he waits "like the groom" (5). His sense of expectation, being likened to that of a bridegroom here, shows that he has fully accomplished his own job of singing the song of hope and survival for his land. Consequently, he foresees "the fullness of a generation in the loin of [his] song" (6). A greater sense of expectation is seen in these metaphors of name: he is "the breakfast glee" (7), the "millet memory" (8), and the "Sorghum son" (8), sown to the land, awaiting the coming of the rain. Here we see the limitation of the singer-persona. While he can prepare his land and himself in expectation of the rain, he has no power to make the rain. He is human like us, but a patriotic one. Verse forty-one intensifies the focus on the land as a prepared bride. "AND SUDDENLY MY LAND BECOMES A BRIDE AGAIN" (1). Is the singer-poet, as a groom, meeting this bride? He romanticises the land "Dressed like the garden of Arcadia" (5). He invokes the mountain and the valleys to the name of the land. He goes on, calling on the fullness of nature:

> Let the evening sun rise in gold, in your name
> Walk in beauty like the deer among hogs
> The forests proclaim your antimony of flesh... (8-10)

The lines above do not only show the beauty of the land, but also the fertility as well as the natural resources the land is endowed with. The singer-persona refers to the land as a "woman, wife, mother, [and] lover..." (11). It is pertinent to mention here that Raji in his recent love poems, both the ones encountered here, and those that have appeared in his poetry column, "Songscape", in a national daily, gives his land a feminine image.[2] The kind of closeness he feels to a woman is what he feels to his land. Thus he is perpetually in love with the land. The reason for this love is seen here:

> For Love is the only language I know
> In a season of parched promises and shrunken memories
> Love is the caprice of remembrance, the remedy of
> Forgetting. (16- 8)

This kind of love heals. Raji considers himself a patriotic poet whose energies are channelled to healing the land of the wounds inflicted on it by the past military dictators. He will not, like many people in the land, dismiss Nigeria and choose to forget her as a nation. Raji's incurable desire to see his land survive and grow against all odds is seen in verse forty-two. He has

> A MOUNTAIN OF DESIRES
> to grow where the rain fails
> to live where death thrives.
> Valleys of valiant longings
> To rise with the beauty of dawn
> To strike Spring where they worship Drought. (1-5)

Nobody can be more sanguine about the survival of his land than the singer-persona here. Even if nature fails him, he still has a hope in the land. The natural phenomena that fail to come today will certainly come tomorrow. This dream of tomorrow, "like a meadow" (8), is inherent in Raji's theme all the time.

The next verse is directed to the inhabitants of the land who may not understand the singer-persona. It appears they have not fully come to team up with him. Hence, he asks

> DO I SPEAK IN SWEAT, SO FURIOUSLY, YOU DON'T
> UNDERSTAND
> Or I speak in song where nobody cares for simple
> symphonies? (1-2)

He keeps (from the beginning of the volume) wondering why they do not understand his course. He laments that "Men have lost all; no flare in their eyes / No eyes in their heads..." (3-4). But he, as a singer, has his eyes, his senses and his voice. Even when people are dying, he thinks and sings of renewal. His testament as a singer of hope is seen in these loaded lines:

> To be counted with the living
> To live in hope and laughter of coming rains
> To take the path of fire and forget despair
> To become finder of footprints and new loves

I make the pledge and think in colours of rebirth
*Nothing's worse than self-inflicted nightmare.* (10-15)

That is why he dreams. He wishes that other men should resurrect from their spiritual deaths and join him in this enterprise of moving the land from the terrible stage of self-inflicted nightmare. In the next verse, he continues to tell us why he sings and cries and sounds *"like the ancient cock"* (10). He says, *"It is because I know all the truth and all the lie"* (12). He understands the land, his lover, more than anyone. It is also the reason he has to discern a dream *"Between darkness and daylight"* (4) and to have to survive and flourish *"between the lovely night and nightmare"* (6). His dream of tomorrow seems to be a potent one. Raji concludes his treatise with natural images that are seasonally there, awakening a man's consciousness to the continuity of life. The singer-persona sees himself thus:

I WILL BE WATER
I will be fire
I will be one with Earth
Where the rainbow breaks
there you will find me
Where the sun strikes there I will be...
When the moon beckons the sea to a duel
Of love, work and play I will be there. (1-8)

He will therefore continue to live. At this time, his voice becomes the voice of the land that is now a new bride. We see the avowal of the land to exist despite all the problems it has gone through. Nigeria is clearly depicted here. Despite the pre- and post-June 12 elections that suffocated the nation with so many wayward, inflammable words and actions, Nigeria continues to exist as one nation even to the chagrin of Nigerians themselves.[3] Lesser problems have torn other countries apart. But Nigeria is resilient in its resolution to be a nation. Raji admires the oneness of Nigeria. And his major thematic concern is to let Nigerians know that the land still has its values; it is still fertile and a fruitful tomorrow is ahead despite the problems Nigeria has gone through. His advice to Nigerians which is seen in the running motif in this volume is this:

Forget the slow faces of sloth and sorrow
Do the work and wait for the laughter of tomorrow. (12-3)

It must be a collective effort. Everyone has to begin to work, not to laze about and lament the plunder of yesterday or the difficulty of today. It is not certain whether the people have taken this advice or not. Raji should have ended the volume the way it begins, bringing in the voices of Takie, Gambia and Asabi (the voices of the people) to react to the songs of the survival and hope sung by the singer-persona. The singer-persona is, in anyway, triumphal in his songs. That he sees himself as a groom and the land as a bride signifies that the land has the hope to survive beyond yesterday and today.

In the latter part of *Lovesong*, Raji fully offers us images that compel our sense of optimism. The poet-persona, emerging as an angry poet from the earlier volumes, now chooses to take a different course, that of persuading his fellow country people to build the shattered land. In spite of his fears that they may not heed his call, he sounds confident and hopeful that his nation shall be free of oppression.

## Notes

1. Up till today there exist Movement for the Actualisation of the Sovereign State of Biafra (MASSOB) demanding for the secession of south eastern Nigeria, and Movement for the Emancipation of the Niger Delta (MEND) demanding for the secession of the Niger Delta area of Nigeria. The legality of these movements, though, are in doubt.
2. Remi Raji, at the time this work is being done, writes a poetry column in *The Sun* newspaper. Entitled "Songscape", most of the poems that appear in it are, like Pablo Neruda's poems, love poems for the poet's country.
3. On June 12, 1993, Nigerians went out en masse to vote late Chief Moshood Abiola as a president. It was said to be the

freest and fairest general elections Nigeria had then, but the then military dictator, General Babangida, annulled the elections to the shock of Nigerians. Thereafter, Nigeria was thrown into chaos as a result of protests and demonstrations.

# CHAPTER
# 6

After his resounding optimism, his shift of metaphors from animal images (used to depict the plunderers) to agrarian images of plantation and germination, dramatising hope, in *Lovesong*, we expect that Remi Raji's next volume will build on the imagery of growth and flourishing; but that is not the case. Indeed the "laughter of tomorrow" Raji foresees in *Lovesong*, his fourth volume of poetry, has become elusive in the fifth volume *Gather My Blood*. Expectedly angst and outrage against the plunderers of his nation return in this volume in an extremely passionate manner. He even slides into pessimism. As it has been clear from our textual explorations that Raji's poetry (except his third volume: *Shuttlesongs America*) moves hand in hand with historical realities in Nigeria, we can, as we had done before, surmise the reason for the intensity of the outrage in this volume. Metaphorically *Lovesong* sees the end of military oppression or, at least, military era in Nigeria. Historically Nigeria attained democracy in 1999 with Olusegun Obasanjo becoming the president. But the democracy was/is so deformed and wonky that it has failed to meet the expectations of Nigerians. *Gather My Blood* evidently contains poems about this post-military era democracy with its disturbing shortcomings. At this point the poet-persona in Raji's poetry is totally frustrated that all the energies he has put into his anti-military songs are in vain, as the civilian regime does not seem better than the military. In this chapter we will examine this level of frustration with the nationalist question, and consider what we may see as the poet's recourse to personal theme, the theme of love, in the face of unending oppression.

*Gather My Blood Rivers of Song*: **Outrage and Epiphany**
As we have demonstrated so far, Raji's finest poems are those
that reverberate with resistance and rage, challenging the myth
of military oppression, and rendering optimism, in the climate of
tender metaphors, to a people torn between survival and death.
*Gather My Blood* also begins with that instinctual concern of the
poet with socio-political issues. Raji's continued engagement with
the political theme exemplifies William Faulkner's opinion that
"the only reason the poet ever writes another poem is that the
one he just finished didn't serve that purpose – wasn't good enough
– so he'll write another one" (quoted in Hersey 31-32). This sense
of longing is imperative in the political poems here; it impels the
poet towards purer, stronger metaphors, and a more discursive
social vision. In the opening poem, "Prologue: I am the million
selves..." Raji's signatures as a political poet present themselves,
and in a range that embraces all strata of the society. At one
point he is the lone speaker in a strange country of "urgent
memoirs" (2), at another point "the cactus tree" (3) with the
names of his country imprinted on its bark; he is also "the sudden
breath of hurricane" (4) with an unconditional love for his
country. In each line, the poet is something else for the sake of his
country, finally seeing himself as "the bruise and the blood from
this stone of a country", a metaphorical definition of a stagnated
Nigeria with an insistent prophet who sees and understands her
unending ailment. In these mutations, the angst and anxiety of
the persona-prophet do not only present him as a resilient
watchman keen about the fate of his country, he undoubtedly
emerges as an enraged town crier with a message that,
interestingly, is both apocalyptic and optimistic. This poem is
exemplary of Raji's discursive social vision in this collection. A
number of overarching images are thrown up. From the flora
and fauna to the elements, from cannibalism to barbarism, from
religion to dogmatism, the disparate images give a sense of the
chaos ravaging Nigeria. In spite of the chaos, the poet-persona
realises that he is still one with the nation. The blood in the

collection's title, then, is akin to the blood in Olu Oguibe's "I am Bound to this Land by Blood". The strong bond between the poet and his society informs the image of blood. For the poet, as Nourbese Philip points out, "the bond between [himself] and [his] place remains indispensable" (174).

"Not a word", more apocalyptic in tone, reverberating with a greater degree of frustration, reads like a poet's last gloomy pronouncement on a dying nation. It is indeed one of the few pronouncements, uncharacteristic of the optimistic poet, that truly express the outrage of a poet-prophet who realises that his message is becoming useless for a nation bound to a moral, ethical and psychic failure. At the beginning, his tone is sober, cowed: "perhaps we are all prisoners of the times" (1). In what follows, the persona, not now a million selves, resigns his fate in a manner that indicates his fruitless efforts in rescuing the failed society. The persona realises, and is helpless about this, that his society is filled with "triumphant fools" (2), "jamming the way to hell" (3), that is, things have gone out of hand so much so that the people are not groping towards light, but receding deeper and deeper into darkness, a certain intensity of the crisis of survival confronting the ordinary people. Typically, the persona, himself a victim of psychological oppression, writes off his land as no longer befitting for human existence. This projection of the nadir of hope does not merely emanate from a hard, critical look at the failed society but it is symptomatic of the gradual breakdown of a national, collective nerve in the face of overwhelming atrocities. For the persona, the thought of remedy, of a positive social change, is a luxury that he does not entertain, and that is why he declares:

> talk to me
> not about
> the peace
> that will soon expire in the hands of inequity,
> and inequality.
> don't tell me
> about your circus

of baldhead buffaloes...
don't preach to me about
unity in the fog of injustice.
I hear the cry too, of men and women
through the years, and of children lost
or drowned in their own bleats... (4-16)

Notice how the stanza appears in the shape of a gun, a symbol of death and waste. The society tortures and kills her children. It is a society where no one asks questions about the oppressed, the maimed and those who "drowned in their own bleats". The metaphors "circus" and "baldhead buffaloes" give us an insight into the kind of ruler-destroyers responsible for the violence in the land. They are Nigerian politicians, who took over from the military, known for their self-indulgent antics, crass opportunism, and a propensity for formulating and implementing policies that are noxious to the less privileged people in Nigeria. Raji is probably having the Obasanjo regime in mind, noted for its dehumanising excesses, and for failing to meet the people's expectations of what a democracy is. We need to properly deconstruct the metaphor "buffaloes" to see how it aptly captures the anti-human tendencies of a pseudo-democracy. Nigerian politicians are fat, overweight, on the side of obesity; their one irrevocable ambition is to feed themselves alone, the grab-all syndrome, insensitive to the hunger and want on the streets; their approach is to pursue aggressively all that benefit them and, strangely too, take a confrontational stand against ideas and actions that will empower the ordinary people in the society. In such a land, the people are repeatedly condemned to a "memory of tears" (19), the nation is laid waste, and the poet is the helpless, frustrated prophet not able to liberate his society.

Raji's outrage running through the poems here stems from the perilous failure of the Nigerian politicians that took over from the military in 1999, a consequence of outrageous greed and aggrandisement. It gradually dawned on Nigerians that the elected politicians – though elections have never been free and fair in

Nigeria – chose to acquire and accumulate wealth instead of serving the society. Beyond that, their ambitions to perpetuate themselves reminded Nigerians of the heinous military regimes that subjected Nigerians to untold hardship. In "Animus I" and "Animus II", Raji pursues the theme of a new kind of oppression, as startling as it seems, in a so-called civilian society where authoritarianism and totalitarianism are too daunting. He begins, in "Animus I", with that characteristic dismal resignation: "I see now we embrace bitterness / like the pill" (1-2). With the collective, victim-defining "we", the poet elaborate what he means by bitterness, defining his nation in stronger, gloomier terms that demands our reassessment of the poet of A Harvest, Webs, and Lovesong, whose political engagement is moulded in incurable optimism, whose heartfelt idiom is the therapeutic laughter. The now outraged poet, in his insistent apocalyptic vision, cuts a picture of an agitated prophet of doom, madly vociferous with a diatribe against the establishment. Thus, the poem is filled with such outbursts:

> Behind the smokescreen
> The silenced dust
> Of detonations I sing
> I cry
> I scream
> I prance
> I pound about... (11-17)

The persona is raging against "this pestilence / of violence and doom" (18-19), the immoral suppression of the poor by the rich, of the ordinary people by the powerful politicians. Each line of this poem screams, howls, and lashes out; each metaphor is a detonation from the talon of a poet extremely infuriated about the plight of the innocent in a society where, as Helon Habila says in Waiting for an Angel, "[the governments] pull down whoever dares to stand up for what is right" (183).

The persona's voice is unrelenting in "Animus II". Harping on a wonky, traded philosophy of nation building, a really parochial and deceitful gospel of nationalism the oppressor-politicians often use to keep the masses perpetually subjugated, Raji questions the sense in asking the people to make sacrifices for their nation when the nation offers in return "a nightmare of skeletons" (18) and "festering litanies of losses" (20). At the same time a few privileged people take over mantle of leadership, "poison the wind" (21) so that the masses are denied free air, and soil their hands in the blood of their neighbours. As in most of the angry poems in this collection, the poet does not see any hope in sight for the battered populace; he rather foresees a society increasingly getting suffocated by an intense condition of totalitarianism. There is just one party in the state: the rich, ruling party, keeping safe in power and taking aggressive measures to remain in power. It is the regime of "the crooks of Unreason" (capital his, 30), where no one ordinary person is free, where the narrative of nationhood is subsumed in self-indulgence and materialism. "Animus I" and "Animus II" are poems of intense feeling, of a broken emotion, the voice harshly penetrative, the diction a piercing dagger of a combatant poet in a last fight against the despoilers of his land. The anger, the rage, overflowing in these poems, as in other poems in this collection, is becoming an enduring characteristic in delineating not only Raji's political poetry, but also the political poetry of his age, possibly because of its historicisation of the worst conditions of living in Nigeria, in addition to the poet's disappointment and mortification over the cyclical, abiku-like nature of oppressive regimes in Nigeria.

It is in fact a moral duty for the poet to be angry. For what else will the poet feel if he is in a land, as we see in "Monotones", that "palpitates...palpitates / like the headless ram" (1-2), whose head is cut off with the knife of oppression. The people are perfectly cowed, becoming "a nation of gangrenous patriots" (8), lacking in direction. The nation is, indeed, a dying one; and the paradox staring at us here is that the oppressor, without knowing it, will end up having no nation to oppress in spite of his innate desire to rule. The relationship between the oppressor and the masses, therefore, is like that of a father that gives his child a serpent as a gift. Raji elaborates this in "Familiar scenes" in which he outlines, through striking symbolism, the features of the oppressor-masses relationship. The oppressor gives the masses a gift of flask "full of serpents" (2); other gifts are a "swine of songs" (4), "a cauldron / of slogans" (5-6), "a drought / of patience" (7-8), and other such gifts that enshrine the superiority of the leader to the led. These gifts, specific symbols of oppression, are meant to keep the populace poor and maimed forever in order that it is easier for the oppressor to keep his powers. The poet here is also worried about the gullibility of the masses which the wicked leaders take advantage of. Easily, the people find themselves, if induced with money and materialism, showering praise songs on the oppressor. They are easily hemmed in by a bouquet of fake but alluring slogans, consequently getting contented with handouts from the leaders and resigning their fate with the injunction, often from a parasitic religious establishment, to remain patient and watch the inevitable passage of time. The poet's summation of this society of inhuman politicians and credulous masses is "A world wedded / to the device of its own calamity" (13-14). Again the catastrophic tone is strong here, the prophecy of doom bodying forth in the nationalist imagination of the once optimistic poet. In the harsh aspect of these poems, Raji is consistently giving the impression that a time comes and the poet-prophet, no matter the degree of his patriotism, no matter the social vision invested in the beloved nation, has to burst out, in the form of forced epiphany, with a cache of metaphors and define his land in realistic terms. Indeed, the imagery here, lucid and tending towards banality, functions as a tool for undressing and exposing the full character of a nation totally adrift. The poet, in this enterprise, is a cousin of the journalist, the self-professed social critic, gnawingly deflecting the immoral, unethical, and corrosive sophistry of the establishment.

   That is what Raji does in "I know the secrets of open roads", specifically focusing on the terrible conditions of roads and road transport in Nigeria. The roads, left unattended to, have become suckers of blood:

> I know the secrets of open roads,
> the pulse of urchins of the blood
> the gash and the gripe of highway paths
> and potholes, I know the secrets of open roads,
> where death hawks her passion per penny. (1-5)

The secrets of the roads are the abiding faith in their resolve to kill those who come upon them. Basically describing the carnage in Nigerian roads, the poem bears strong metaphors that take our attention beyond the roads to the authorities that are in charge of the roads. The state of Nigerian roads has been a great source of concern for the citizenry; the poet, with his army of metaphors, is indeed echoing the outcries of Nigerians over the deplorable conditions of the roads. Road accidents are daily occurrences, but the more agonising aspect of it is that the authorities do not care, possibly because they travel by air, which is why "the road bleeds and the bleeding is unending" (16). The pervasive carnage fills the society with "the sodom smell of things" (19), making the poet-persona uncomfortable. This vivid portrayal of the Nigerian roads, the road transport being the major transport system in Nigeria, further reveals the insecurity of life and properties in a country that is said to be the giant of Africa. From all angles, the masses are faced with hardship and other terrible conditions that even result to death. The poet, in a tone of frustration, wonders what kind of land he lives in, he is appalled that human lives can be so wantonly wasted and even celebrated: "I can taste the blood-breath of flying roads / the last fragrance of flowers in mourning" (8-9). There is nothing to live for in this country except death, not the death that comes from the roads alone, but also deaths from all other strata of the society. One remarkable, though disturbing, thing that goes with Raji's rage in this collection is the concentrated imagery of death running through almost all the poems. Almost at the core of every image in each poem is death, not uncanny, spiritualised and celebratory, as in the poetry of the Malagasy poet, Jean-Joseph Rabearivelo (see, for instance, Ulli Beier 89-94), but the death of war and waste, indeed the fatal consequence of the inordinate passion of Nigeria's oppressors, not military as in Raji's earlier volumes, but civilian, for watching while the Nigerian masses die of suffering, hunger and state-organised killings. At another level, then, blood is a metaphor of waste. This double-edged deployment of metaphor is not new in Raji's poetry: in his earlier works laughter is both seen as a balm and as a weapon of mockery.

Organised and (extra-)judicial killing is the thematic focus of "Somewhere, she shall be stoned to death...", a poem written about Amina Lawal, a woman from northern Nigeria condemned to death by stoning in a sharia court of law. Amina Lawal faced the wrath of the Islamic sharia law in Funtua, Katsina State, because she gave birth to a baby out of wedlock. In the poem, Raji, in a satiric pitch, raises issues on the hypocrisy beneath the sharia legal system; the double standards and pretentious nature of its practitioners; and the excesses, anti-human, of the Islamised Katsina State where Amina Lawal was convicted. The poet-persona is clearly on the side of the woman, empathising with her for being caught in the web of religio-human egos displayed by a highly patriarchal system. The fundamental issue that bothers the poet is that it takes two to commit adultery, but it is the woman that is facing the law. The absence of the male suspect in the poem implies that all males, including the shari'a judges are responsible for Amina Lawal's pregnancy. The poet, through the images of death and blood, engages the conscience of the condemners, elevating the woman to the status of a martyr. "Her blood", the poet says, "shall water the parched penitence / of perpetual pretenders" (2-3). Repeating the phrase, "She shall be stoned to death", in a tone sounding both satiric and supplicatory with the diction filled with future tenses indicating the consequences of the inhuman action, the poet-persona speaks of how the blood of the woman, not that of the man with whom she makes love, will disturb the phallo-centric self-image of the society symbolised in "man's reckless groin" (5), "the urine of vampires" (13), "the ash of pretence" (15), and "the pretender stone" (18). Infused in this poem is the biblical allusion of the death and resurrection of Christ: the poet persona says the woman shall be stoned to death and "On the third day, she shall rise / from the dust, from the ash of our pretence" (14-15). After that

> The stones shall become diamonds
> and rumours, rubies around her waist
> When she survives the pretender stone
> her story shall be distilled into the land
> as the salience of salt. (16-22)

This then is the effectuation of her metamorphosis into a martyr. Here, she acquires a personality that is overtly superior to those of her would-be killers. This, to some extent, is prophetic on the Amina saga because after the outcries that follow her conviction, Nigeria did not hear again of any other woman subjected to such humiliation; in fact, the worth of the sharia system dwindled; political sentiments and undertones, manifested in the hypocritical activities of the leaders, were detected in the system.[1]

In "Ode to torch bearers", Raji turns his attention to the Nigeria police, unveiling, as it were, the many infamies of the law enforcement agency in a criminally despoiled nation. Some of these infamies treated in this poem include: the massive corruption in the police, the open cowardice, the crass display of inexperience, of the police in dealing with criminals in the society, the extortion of the innocent people on the roads, and raw violence as when innocent people are shot for refusing to bribe the police. These problems combine to give the police a terribly bad image in Nigeria. The Nigeria police had acquired notoriety for supporting violence, crime and corruption instead of standing against them. Beyond that, the Nigeria police, because of its tainted image, came to be synonymous with some kind of underdog authority to the extent that people avoided coming in contact with the police. In this poem, Raji constructs his imagery with "torch", a favourite instrument of the police while on night patrol. The torch is essential in the sense that without it the police are blind to crimes; they need the torch to be able to see, to uncover criminal activities in every nook and cranny of the society. Indeed, the torch is a symbol of insight, comprehension and vision for the police, as it leads them into the night and into the darker things of life. But that is not what a torch is to the Nigeria police. For them, the torch is not an instrument to fight crimes, but to commit crimes; it is one for extorting the road users. The police, as dramatised by the poet here, are notorious for mounting a roadblock with "drums" (1) at the "junctions" (2), flashing their torches at the drivers and passengers on the road and demanding bribes from them after ascertaining that they are ordinary people, not big politicians or their superior officers. The persona addresses the police: "I am surprised by your sleight of hands, your drunken pose / on afflicted roads, your scowl, your glare in dark and daylight" (5-6). The picture here is not that of a composed security officer ready to face the challenges of securing the life and property of the people in the society. The police's sleight of hands denote their propensity for bribe taking in a brazen manner on the roads; their "scowl" and "glare" are what they use to intimidate the poor people in order to extort money from them. The persona then throws insults at the police: "The unpredictable ember of stray violence / the plain majesty of foulness, ah the friendly foe..." (7-8). In spite of their pervasive corruption and uncontrolled violence against the less privileged in the society, the Nigeria police see themselves as friends of the masses. It is a slogan they exhibit everywhere in Nigeria, even though Nigerians do know that the last person they can go to in the case of violation of their rights is the policeman. The persona, still addressing the police with virulent words, says, "I fear the logic of your gun, arrogant before the hapless" (9). He accuses the police of conniving with armed robbers to render the society unsafe for the masses; he accuses the police of not only being "kitted like the tattered rat" (11) but of also behaving like the rodents, emphasising here on the nature of rodents to steal and destroy. The persona concludes by saying,

When next my daughter wonders
why your pocket bursts with your victim's sweat

I will tell her the tale of torchbearers
who only have darkness to share. (12-16)

The paradox is piercing. Each line of the poem, as we have seen, is venomous, projecting the voice of the poet in a state of tantrum, attacking the enemies of his nation which is very dear to him. In his political poems, Raji has endeavoured to give such confrontation to all unbecoming strata of the Nigerian polity, to unsettle and ruffle the establishment of inept and corrupt practices, especially as they directly affect the lives of the common people. This has been at the core of his marrying poetry to nationalism, of being on the side of "the people in their endless parley with those chosen or imposed as their leaders" (Abdu xii).

In "Song of Toronto", it is the political class that Raji confronts. The background to this poem is an event that took place in 1999, when Nigeria freshly transited from prolonged military regime to civilian government. A vibrant, eager-to-lead young man, Salisu Buhari, was elected in the House of Representatives as the Speaker. He had barely spent a few months, when it was uncovered that he had a fake certificate of a degree from University of Toronto, Canada. Mr Buhari was disgraced out of the office. Thereafter there was a spate of startling discoveries concerning the pretentious and bogus lives of Nigerian politicians. Cases of forgery and impersonation among Nigerian politicians are still current issue in Nigeria today. Spurred by the Salisu case, Raji wrote this poem to satirise, in essence, the insincerity, hypocrisy, and the subsequent failure of politicians in Nigeria today. Raji deploys two devices to a greater degree here: hyperbole and alliteration. Beneath every alliterative, knifing metaphor is a hyperbole, achieving the effect of satire. He allows the politicians to speak, to give life in the form of bizarre words to their shameless acts. The poem begins with the persona saying,

My certificate is long, VERY L-O-N-G

> Broader than your homegrown degree
> It is all wrapped and rolled
> in an ocean of colours.... (Capitals his, 1-4)

This at once reveals the boastful nature of Nigerian politicians. Really, the impersonator-politician believes a degree from Toronto, from Western nations, is superior to the one obtained in Nigeria, even though he is not concerned about the collapse of educational institutions in Nigeria. The first line, and the emphasis here is on "long", also shows the foolish politician who thinks Toronto is such a far place from Nigeria that it might not be easy to detect the forgery. The entire poem is cast in this structure of boasting, of self-damaging revelation which the poet carefully negotiates from a sombre confession. Apart from being "Minted in Minsk / Made in Madagascar / Brought from Bermuda" (5-7), the fake politician boasts of other higher degrees in order to inflate his ego, to move in the circle of the intellectually accomplished in the society. Asserting the extraordinariness, the esoteric prowess, of his degrees, he informs us of his highest achievement:

> Fresh from Tokyo
> A baccalaureate of Rio
> Science major from Chicago
> And Ph.D. General from Toronto. (13-16)

Each line above is shorter than the one below it; that is how each paper qualification is stronger, expected to be more influential, than the one before it; that is how the impersonator-politician desires to grow stronger in knowledge and influence without the pains of going to school. As if the paper qualification has enormous influence in the performance of the politicians in the House, his assumption is that with such degrees, he "will rule the air" (17), he will intimidate others with "a riot of speeches at the fair!" (18), and his "glamour [will dwarf] the jealous and the sick" (20). That the impersonator-politician is interested in forging those degrees only to accomplish what he states above indicates the senselessness of the Nigeria politicians in public dealings and their unrestrained passion for mere exhibitionism. It also points to the fact, which is Raji's underlying message in this poem, that the politicians are not out to work to the benefit of the nation; in fact, they do not even know how to use their offices to bring development to the nation. With his degrees, the impersonator-politician has learnt to "make promises that wake the dead" (21). It is such promises one finds in the land where such politicians are in powers. The voice that replies the impersonator-politician, which apparently is the voice of the poet-persona, paints even gloomier pictures of the political system in the land. According to the voice, the politician does not need to go as far as Toronto or elsewhere to get forged degrees, he can get worst things such as an "honorary doctor of Kleptosophy / in the nearby private tower behind the bush" (44-45). Raji may have coined the word "Kleptosophy" by joining the word "kleptomania" and "philosophy", which captures the driving force behind every politician's ambition in Nigeria. According to the poet, the impersonator-politician does not even need a degree to be an active member of the political class in Nigeria, "Where cash is the grammar of class" (37). The poet here zeroes in on the most alarming crime of the Nigerian politicians against the populace, namely the looting and sharing of huge funds which ought to be directed towards positive developments in the nation. During the Obasanjo regime spanning 1999 to 2007, Nigerian parliamentarians were incessantly accused of siphoning public funds and of only fighting for issues that concern their allowances and more money for themselves. They grew disproportionately rapacious, drawing hues and cries from Nigerians who felt betrayed by them. Today in Nigeria when people seek elections into the National Assembly, and indeed to any position in Nigeria, they are said to be seeking for an opportunity to go take their share of the national cake. This, generally, is what politics, politicking and elections have been reduced to in Nigeria. This is the philosophy of kleptomania the poet refers to as "kleptosophy". Though Raji, in this poem, does not in his characteristic tantrum explode with vituperation on the politicians, the satire, cast in dialogism, is a more potent indictment of the political class for working against the Nigerian nationhood.

With these poems, angrier than the poems of the earlier collections, Raji appears to have hit utter frustration about his nation. There are poems, though, that give us a glimpse of his signature optimism. They are however overshadowed by this intense rage orchestrated in greater tenor in this volume.

## In Time of Hate: Love, Angst, and Triumph

The theme of love is not new to Raji's poetry; there are love poems in his first and second collections. In *Lovesong*, love is the idiom that offers a nuanced terrain for Raji to relay the poetics of nationalist reconstruction. In *Gather My Blood*, however, Raji is eclectic with love in a sustained range, and in a fashion that goes beyond the "publicness" of the idiom in *Lovesong*; he returns, in diverse tones and tenors, to the anguish of flesh desirous of communion. In *Lovesong* his idiom is overtly public, nationalistic, cultural, and psychical; in *Gather My Blood* love defies the confinement of idiom, often spills to *literal* fleshly domain: the subject is not a nation but a woman although the figure of woman here is susceptible to multi-layered interpretations. What is of interest to us here, and which fits into the programmatic design of Raji's persistent political tenor, is the disturbing, *anxious* interstice between the man, really the persona, and the woman in which Raji attempts to locate the crisis of nationhood, and the quest for a liberated selfhood. The central argument here, then, is that Raji's love poems in *Gather My Blood* are personal on the surface but beneath them there is the political question of being, of survival, of triumph. The love in these poems is located in the time of hate (the tension between the leader and the led), of struggles, of survival; and the love becomes an added anxiety in a climate of self-realisation; it generates angst out of which the persona emerges tortured but triumphal.

The opening line of "Dreamtalk" sets out the desire that anticipates the angst which results from the difficulty that runs through the poem: "I will like to turn you inside out and step into your skin". From a man to a woman, or vice versa (or in a same sex circumstance), if in the mood of love, this sounds as easy as climbing the bed and feeding off each other's sexual flesh. It is surely a metaphorical invitation to lovemaking. But this invitation is only a prelude to the complex drama the poem enacts, which, if carefully understood, stretches beyond the mere game of lovemaking. As in most of Raji's love poems, the characters are the bare "I" and "You", almost proving genderless. There is nothing lexically suggesting that "I" is a man and "You" a woman, or vice versa. If we resort to the sociology of the poem (that the poem, like all of Raji's poems, is rooted in the Yoruba tradition) or if we resort to the psychology of the author (that Raji as a poet does have, *love*, a wife; or is known to have female friends; that his mind is attuned to man-woman affair), then we can safely read "Dreamtalk" as a dramatisation of an unstable affair between a man, the "I" of the poem, and a woman, the "You" of the poem.

Any sociological reading will surely support the persuasive, wooing, almost kowtowing voice of the persona which continues to unfold with greater zest throughout the poem. In the Yoruba society, in most if not all African societies, the woman, even if she will later live an unpleasant life in the man's house, enjoys, during declaration and courtship, the sweet and small talks of love from the man. "Dreamtalk" is all about these talks, ascending the plain, transcending metaphors. The persona is wooing a woman, a task that seems to prove impossible, climaxing in (even to the reader) an unsatisfactory and frustrating end. The persona, the male of this affair, persuades, cajoles, entices, promises, and attempts ceaselessly to baulk the shifting movements of a supposed lover. He knows her problem: "And because you shift, you shift, you shift and shift / I can tell you cringe to see the hypnosis of your own silence" (15-16). Her cyclical shifting and her disturbing silence are two of her habits that anchor the conflict of this poem, which spurs the reader to want to probe into issues beyond the act of shifting and silence.

But the poem itself, like the woman being wooed, is enigmatic. There is a certain abstraction, a fluidity, to the poem; an ungraspable misdirection that seems to motivate its course. The lovers lack a background: we know nothing about their identities; nothing to show they are either coming back after a break up or beginning a relationship. But we can glean that in stanza ten when the persona says: "And because ours is a deep-scarred cataract of anguish / I will love you still in this age of hate and cholera" (20-21). Here is revealed a temporality that is in consonance with the historicism underlying the thematic substance of Raji's political poetry. The anguish, interestingly felt by the two lovers-to-be, is located in a time of oppression captured in the phrase "hate and cholera" (notice its echoing of Gabriel Gercia Marquez's *Love in the Time of Cholera*). The anguish then is not that of the man alone but that of the woman too; it suggests therefore that the woman's action is surely motivated by external forces that are potential enemies to the couple-to-be. If at all they surpass these enemies, i.e. if the woman realises her voice and stops shifting, they will emerge as a symbol of a future for their nation, as it were, doomed with hate and cholera. In his pleading, straining voice, the persona says: "We will dream dreams and our dreams will become / The cushion stones of new times, new seeds, new fruits" (38-39). This is envisioning a bright future for themselves, their posterity (if there is ever going to be any), and their society. But, alas, this appears fruitlessly utopian, as the persona moans: "Our dream, my dream, but where are you in this trance / I will go back to the crossroads I'm sure you're waiting..." (40-41). The suggestion here that he will find her at the crossroads is clearly deceptive.

The indefiniteness of this poem is complicated by its hallucinatory tone. This may be understood if it is really a *literal* dream talk (from its title Dreamtalk) where a hurt lover is caught in one of his fits of outburst. Whichever way the poem is viewed, it is clear that the poem bears a certain thematic weight. It is an entire rhetoric of love and self-subjection, but one that inescapably lengthens to the domain of human contradictions. Raji is deliberately loquacious in the poem, the rhetoric veering, among other things, into issues of love and romance, of life and death, of violence ("hidden bleeding images" (4)) and instability, of religion and spirit, and of science and philosophy. This also constitutes the strength of the poem in displaying a rare level of anguish and angst. We see the persona thrashing from one metaphor to another, desperate to claim or reclaim this lover who continues to shift and elude him like "the extra day in a leap year" (14). While the poet represses the voice of the sought lover, it may be wrong to conjecture that she does not love the man; what the poem rather suggests is that the present condition of life, the current state of anomy, is one that defies love; something other than mere wooing commands love in a time of anguish and hate.

Perhaps a stronger poem along that line is "Whisper in the silence" – stronger because it seems more concrete, and elaborates more on the crisis of survival that forms a background to the rupture depicted. In this poem the lover-persona, too, is a man, identifiably a writer. He also woos and makes promises, though not as sweet-tongued as the persona of "Dreamtalk". The dour atmosphere is heavier in this poem, and there are more concrete references to a state of anomy. The lover-persona in the beginning compares himself to a balloon "In the sensation of dangerous knowing" (3), drawing our attention to the uncertainty that confronts him as he makes to venture into a sphere of love. This seems like a cautious step, already anticipating any eventualities. In the following stanza he declares: "I shall write predictable lines that cry for consummation" (5). These lines, as he goes on to unveil, betray a happening that prefaces this love poem, which is that a friction had earlier occurred between the persona and his lover, necessitating this somewhat act of suturing.

But this poem too is slippery. Raji injects an incredible dose of indeterminacy into his love poems in *Gather My Blood* either to conceal, to becloud, or to pluralise issues that will otherwise neatly underline the poet's private life. He therefore lays side by side images of beauty and ugliness, of love and hate, of life and death. So in the persona's "predictable lines" there will be themes of "lust and the story of blood" (7), and of "forgiving, forgetting, forsaking, foreboding, forewarning" (8). But, more importantly, the persona is set to be brave all through the unfolding drama of finding and getting back the lover. The lover-persona already lives in a harsh condition:

> And I, surprised at the deft cruelness of guided exile
> Walking through the corridors of cold stares, still
> I am here, dreadlocked, in an open space, an invisible wall
> Solid as glass, my fingers find your face, but you are far
> away. (9-12)

Exile and alienation, inclement weather, an unkempt body, and a houseless condition characterise the plight of the lover-persona in spite of, because of, which he yearns to reconcile with the lover. Which is why he pens the "predictable lines" to her. Soon the image of the lover's face "screaming back" suggests that the anguish is deeper than what we think. The overall picture of the persona's lover we have is that she is angry, petulant and will not be moved by the poetry of apology reaching her from the lover-persona.

It therefore dawns on the lover-persona that he may have been making all the efforts in vain. Frustratingly he asks: "Will my voice thus grate in vain?" (25). Through a number of rhetorical questions his plaintive voice reaches the end of his song, which obviously does not yield a response from the lover. His voice in the last stanza of the poem is strained, finally pleading with the woman, the lover, to cast him into "the sea of forgetting" (34) so that he can be free. But this is ironic. Throughout the poem, the voice of the woman, as in "Dreamtalk", is unheard, and it seems clear that the lover-persona, even from the beginning of the poem, is set on a fruitless venture. He possibly cannot reclaim the woman; he is exiled, alienated. Exile here could be metaphorical, capturing the gap between him and the lover artificially created in the climate of despondency in which they live. As in "Dreamtalk" the poem ends with a heightened sense of pessimism.

The poem "Echo", if read after "Dreamtalk" and "Whisper in the silence", comes through as the eventuality resulting from the unyielding stance, as it were, of the female lover being wooed back. Expectedly the tone becomes grimmer, sadder, *excruciatingly* pessimistic. The lover-persona's voice slides from the level of persuasion into that of painful resignation; his mood is characterised by the morose and suicidal feeling that come with the harshness of unrequited love. The image of the departing sun and the image of solitude which open the poem set the rather drastically urgent tone of the poem. The lover-persona knows it is all over, or about to be so, and he is at that critical junction where a supposedly jilted lover (i.e. himself) must stab the conscience of the heartless partner who defies all entreaties. This is what Raji achieves with this poem. Carefully – mercilessly – marshalling one provocative image after another, Raji constructs a drama of conscience in which the (now self-important) lover-persona is in his final act of disengagement.

The lover-persona begins his address to his lover with a touching line: "Now I leave you with a sensation as of a lover's departing night" (4). Notice that this echoes the previous sweet nights they may have had together; it engages memory and is aimed at unsettling the poise of the heartless partner. The attack on her conscience becomes harsher in the next line: "And the last echoes of your depraved anger follow me" (6). This is resoundingly judgemental. At once, the lover-persona wants us to believe that his (female) partner, the heartless one, is responsible for this break up. It is the petulant, unreasonable, unyielding, lover of "Whisper in the silence" that surfaces here. The lover-persona is not yet done, as he launches another salvo: "The cloud here is not poisoned like the ether in your face" (8). He goes on to speak of the "mud, sling and snake in [her] belly" (9); he talks of her "depraved tongue" (11); and he boasts of surviving not just in the climate of her *depraved* attitude but also – and this is how Raji blends personal and social issues – in the season of wanton deaths in his society. He is being jilted in an oppressive society: he is therefore faced with a double-headed depression. There is a real sense in which the lover-persona, instead of attracting our sympathy, incurs our hatred upon himself for being judgementally and sentimentally self-loving. This is the kind of lover-persona one encounters in Uche Nduka's *Heart's Field*, utterly self-centred, self-justifying, and vulgarly anti-feministic.

But perhaps the point of divergence between Uche Nduka's lover-persona and Raji's lover-persona here is that while the former chuckles through his enterprise (Uche Nduka's humour silently reverberates through his uncompromising formalism), the latter is clearly mired at the crossroads where it seems to him that the best path to take is to disengage from the lover, and the decision itself does not come easy for him. He bursts out appealingly: "But I love you still..." (11); he wishes that she were not what she is; he is even ready to endure further, bragging that "I survive...where love has no name" (12). It is however clear towards the end of the poem that this strained, frustrating outburst (i.e. the entire poem) is being made when it is clear that the lover-persona has lost this lover. That is why finally he says, "I always remember the days of tears. I remember you" (15). The metonymic depth of "tears" here is better imagined, especially giving the *angst* of the lover-persona in the preceding poems, "Dreamtalk" and "Whisper in the silence".

The lover-persona in the poem "A sacrament" speaks with a less pained, more relaxed voice. The loss is there but the anger is suppressed. Here he flings no invectives at the gone lover although he continues, as incurably as ever, his self-portrayal as the *lover* of the affair, i.e. the one who loves, whose love is unreturned. The images here are affectionate and the achieved tone almost evokes sympathy in us. This poem too is an act of memory:

> You left with the blood in my tongue on your lips
> I still see the lushness of your eyebrows.

I could pick that valiant stub of shining hair. (1-3)

Deliberately, of course, the image of blood is positioned in the first line to remind us of the violence, both physical and psychological, running through this love poem, and others. We have already been familiar with the angry and depraved lover, who may have in a fit of argument struck the lover-persona, who indeed has heartlessly abandoned the lover-persona in spite of all the petitions. Going with the blood of the lover-persona in her lips can also suggest that she has taken advantage of him, has bruised his soul despite his kindness, and has left him in a manner that shows she has no conscience. This interpretation is supported by the next stanza where the lover persona says, "I felt the mint of your prayers; and when I kissed your foot / it was for the remembrance of the pact with your soul" (4-5). Surely it takes a knight of a man, especially in Africa, to kiss a woman's foot, if we choose to look at the line *literally*. But as a metaphor the implication is weightier, and suggests the deep, unquantifiable love and protection that the lover-persona offers his lover. The pact he has with her soul is to love her, to care for her, to protect her as his "archangel of spicy sensation" (10). That is why when she jilts him, "The ground beneath [her] grace quivered with my tears" (6). Notice that this hyperbole is syntactically constructed in the past; this means they have broken up, i.e. this poem, like "Echo", is a remembrance that betrays the inerasable desire of the lover-persona to have her back. He praises her beauty, recognises her overwhelming influence on him, and seems now to be content that she has returned to him "as a dream" (13). Her image is bold before him. What he remembers of her is "the good habit of [her] heart" (19), quite unlike the lover-persona of "Echo". But the sense of loss and cessation is profound.

In the poem "Scent", it is to the sensuous that Raji first appeals. As the title implies the lover-persona lives with the scent of the woman with whom he once shares "familiar sounds" (3). With her scent and her image hovering around he lacks sleep, he is perpetually condemned to the "midsummer moments" (5) of the beach where he ceaselessly agonises her disappearance. The tone of this poem is weepy, the loss reverberating through every image. Its sadness is intensified by the subtle Rajian political theme running through it. The lover-persona confesses that he needs his lover with whom it will be easier to pass through this moment of oppression and depression. The image of the sea cutting across the poem clearly suggests the endlessness of the lover-persona's grief, the uncertainty and indeterminacy facing his life. While he consoles himself that the "memory of [his lover's] breath" will see him through the hard time, he quickly recalls how it had been when she was with him. But now his life, his society, is besieged by the "relentless rite of riggers" (11), by which he means the rigging and corruption that make nonsense of the nascent democracy in his country. Concentrating more on the hardship, he talks of people living "like phantoms" (13), lacking a direction, sunk into the despair that comes with instability, an instability, along with a confusion, cushioned by the "fast slogans" (14) of mindless politicians. The sense one has of this poem, as one reaches beyond the images, is that the lover-persona and his lover did live fighting for a political change only for it to come but in the shape of slogans and "fondling and fencing" (12) words; and at this time, to add salt to injury, the lovers have broken up (or the lover has died, as the absence here, perhaps because of the weepy tone of the poem, sounds like death). The "we" of the poem is certainly not of the two lovers, but the entire society on behalf of whom the lover-persona laments, "we have survived too long" (13); they are no longer ready to live or die by slogans alone. In the interface between the loss of the woman and the loss of his society's dream, the lover-persona's tone becomes revolutionary, pointing to the possibility of his fighting for the society on behalf of his lost lover.

The elaborately titled poem "A lifer looks at his woman's photo, from a prison window..." reads like a sequel to "Scent". This is not to say the poet intends it to be so. The thematic link between the poems, indeed among all the poems discussed here, forms the basis for that claim. The lover-persona is now, finally, in prison; nothing in the poem to show why he is in prison. But it does seem that given his anguish and diversely manifested angst towards his unbending mistress and corrupt society, prison comes as a natural home for him. In a sense he has been living in an ambience of imprisonment, perpetually subjected to the unpleasant enterprise of winning back a rigid lover. What is even more interesting now is that being behind bars does not release him from that ambience of imprisonment; and he tenaciously gives us the impression that the prison condition of wooing back the woman is self-given.

Here too, as in the previous poems, the lover-persona talks to his invisible lover. Starting from her speech, what he calls "[her] lines" (1), he describes his lover, concentrating on her erogenous parts such as her breasts, her long hair and her laps. The dominant tone here is that of worshipping; the lover-persona seeks to give us a transcendental image of beauty and sex. It is an image he also constructs for himself, to offer him succour, as paradoxical as it seems, in this climate of chaining. With her milky honey of lines, with the "poetry" (5) in her eyes, with her "breathless breasts" (7), and the "depth" (10) of her laps, all coming back to him in a constant stream of memory, the burden of the prison becomes lighter. The climax of this imagining is to have their "bodies breathe again... / to part no more" (15). This is no doubt illusory, and like most illusory things, offers him a ground for daydreaming, for occasionally escaping the reality in which he finds himself. Perhaps this stage of illusoriness in the saga of the lover-persona comes naturally after his enduring but ineffective litany of entreaties. Beyond consoling himself with the image of his lover – may be that same lover that eludes him, the lover-persona realises the power of poetry, of words, which can heal the kind of psychological wound that the lover-persona is inflicted with. Thus the poetry he glimpses in her eyes, that ritual of words that will inevitably cushion his pains in the prison, forms the thematic base of the poem "Words can heal".

"Words can heal", as the title makes clear, is a poem in which the lover-persona dishes for himself the therapy that results from a humanistic word-craft. It has all the characters of the earlier poems regarding the lover-persona's loquacity, his un-displaced ego, his tenacity, but, above all, his realisation, finally, that he (but also she and the entire world) need the healing a word can give. This seems practical than giving himself up for any urge for suicide that often comes upon failed lovers. With this we can buttress our earlier conjecture that the lover-persona is himself a writer, a poet, who is also a great lover chasing after a love of his heart. His assured voice here, almost as of a teacher to a student, and his downright philosophisation show his sense of involvement in the art of poetry. For him, "tender metaphors" (2) are the wools to dress "The wound of a thousand years..." (1), a hyperbole that may remind us of his prolonged pain and sense of neglect as a rejected lover. He repeats, "Words can heal the pain of a lifetime" (3). This, if it is about healing himself or getting his lover to forgive whatever wound he has inflicted on her, is also a piece of advice that is intended for anyone in the society. Indeed there is a social sense to this: poetry, for most poets from struggling societies, should be a stream of words aimed at healing the wound of a contradicted life.

Typical of Raji's love poems in this volume, this poem, in spite of its philosophical weight, does not shy away from that recurrent theme of wooing. Beneath some of the lines that sound like universal statements the lover-persona is in fact taking a circuitous way to soften the heart of his lover. One of such is: "Words can make love to bleeding hearts / And the most granite of looks can fail / In the presence of wondrous words" (4-6). The rigid stance of the wooed lover perhaps have necessitated this seemingly general statement. There is implicit in this statement a desire to get back a "granite" look and to heal a bleeding heart, bleeding here of course referring to the kind of personal chasm that occurs between two lovers. He goes on to say that "And when everything else fails / We turn to the windy poetry of words" (11-

12). This is a turning point. The futility of continued wooing has already stared him in the face, and resorting to poetry, a windy one for that matter, is to continue to have faith in the possibilities, such as dialogue, that speech offers. The image of wind is to be stressed in the final line of the poem: "Woman, wear the wind like the winsome night" (15). With the wind the lover-persona hopes that the woman, the lover, will move in a direction not of her volition; winds can powerfully move a mind in any direction. A windy poetry then is one that is expected to sweep the woman off her feet and put her in the imagined space the lover-persona has for her. This poem, swinging between philosophical words intended for the reader and a subtle message, as it were, intended for his *lost* woman, is a possible ending for the angst that characterise the utterances of the lover-persona in the earlier poems.

In spite of the angst, the one-sided anguish, the failed rhetoric of love, the lover-persona feels a sense of triumph in such poems as "Return", "Beyond the blues" and "Aftersong". Not that he is extricated from the bondage of love. But as he says in "Return":

...I am the patient spider
of sinister days, only the dream never died
though it has paled to a faint period...
I return, to labour and, to love. (6-9)

He is still the lover but now his ego surpasses the pessimism of the moment; he will no longer be the pleading, suppliant, even piteous, man after a lover that will not listen to him. The dream to reclaim the woman is still there but he is no longer a prisoner of that dream. "Aftersong" is cast in the idiom of freedom. The freedom is presented as a puzzling realm which, no matter what, has to be attained. It is what the lover-persona, at least after the turbulence he has passed through, desires. But it is, according to him, "a season away" (5); freedom is "the rains after the dragon's / blood" (6-7). Raji switches to his political theme here, using "dragon" to represent the oppressor of his nation. It is when the oppressor is killed, perhaps violently in a revolution, that there will be genuine freedom. "Beyond the blues" is explicitly political, almost having no images of love, but a keen reader will see that the persona is the failed lover who has now chosen to "labour" and yet not to stop loving. Like the combative persona of Raji's political poems, the lover-persona here, "Already soaked in rivers of aches" (9), speaks of revolutionary dreams for a just society:

> I dream
> about redolent nights
> when thunder will speak
> for hopeless orphans on threatened roads
>
> I dream
> of tomorrow's rainbow's call
> when leopards will leap
> in the sun of spotless laughters.
> I dream
> until this eclipse dies
> to the rays of a new anthem. (13-23)

In this body of dreams is encompassed a triumph with which the lover-persona returns to life. It is perhaps easier at this point to dream of a socialist intervention than to dream of an amorous adventure, which, as we have seen so far, does not yield any result. This is pertinent because, with the hints in some of the poem, it does appear that the woman's love for him is hamstrung by some social constraints. It is not that the woman gives her heart to another man; it is not that she expresses any personal dislike for him. He therefore seems, right from the outset, to be working against the tide of an unfavourable social matrix. This is the "eclipse" whose end he foresees; and the rise of "a new anthem" is certainly a metaphorical representation of the bliss that a perfect love affair, perhaps when hate and cholera have passed, will bring.

These and other poems in *Gather My Blood* all prove that even as the enraged poet *withdraws* into a privatist space, having been a frustrated town crier, he cannot totally divorce his voice from an engagement with his nation. Our conclusion is that there is something *inherently* political even in Raji's un-political poems.

**Notes**

1. Started in Zamfara State in northern Nigeria, some northern Nigerian states adopted the sharia legal system in such a dramatic way that for quite some time the sharia issue became a dominant social discourse in Nigeria. However, the Amina Lawal conviction in 2002 exposed the wicked face of the sharia system, drawing loud outcries against it. Baoba for Women's Human Rights, a Nigerian NGO, took up Amina Lawal's case; several contestants of the Miss World Beauty Contest slated to take place in Nigeria threatened to boycott the event in support of Amina Lawal. The Oprah Winfrey Show had a report on Amina Lawal and encouraged US citizens to send emails to the Nigerian government on behalf of Amina Lawal and over 1.2 million emails were sent. The sharia system in Katsina State had to upturn Amina Lawal's case.

# CHAPTER
# 7

After *A Harvest* and *Webs of Remembrance*, two collections intensely realised through the nationalist imagination, Remi Raji published *Shuttlesongs America*, a kind of poetic travelogue that captures his first trip to the United States of America. Our location of the discourse on this volume in this chapter is deliberate, as it only marginally fits into the programmatic design of this book. Like most travelogues the volume recollects landmark objects and events in the poet's sojourn and, as a work of imagination, foregrounds the contradictions (in matters of race, identity, and migration) in the American society. Although it lacks the venomous tone of the earlier collections, or the ones after it (serving here as a temporary break from Raji's master-theme, as it were), *Shuttlesongs America* also offers Raji the wherewithal to compare the American society and his own society with the result that he becomes even more attached to his nation. Our concern in this chapter is to delve into the multi-layered, though arguably loose, images the poet offers us in this volume.

### *Shuttlesongs America: A Poetic Guided Tour*: Beyond the Shores of Nigeria

In *Shuttlesongs America* Raji's thematic concern is not about the problems of Nigeria, his dear country, although Nigeria is implicitly embedded in the texture of the volume. The nationalist imagination is, from the context of racism, palpable in it. It is not only in the landscape of theme that this volume differs from others of Raji's collections, but also in the sphere of style. Raji's poetry here descends from the too serious height of African poetry to embrace the soft diction and imagery of American poetry. The poetry of this collection is so soft and audience-friendly that the author, in its defence, says it is packaged as a poetic guide for those who may want to see parts of America in poetry or share their experiences with that of Raji whose first visit to the USA spurred it. It is written in American English, unlike other collections. *Shuttlesongs America* is thus distinguished from Raji's earlier collections in its language and its somewhat peculiar cover design. Talking of his language and style in this collection, Raji says:

> The images are simple. I ... had a different audience in mind when I was writing it. I wanted people to read it without having metaphors as a wedge between reading and understanding. The metaphors there are, however, not watery. They are subterranean. (*The Ker Review*, 78)

Indeed in terms of imagery and symbolism a reader familiar with Raji's concrete and captivating images and symbols in his previous collections will be disappointed with the imagistic weakness of *Shuttlesongs America*, in spite of the rationale given above. Audience patronisation, no matter the motive behind it, is one of the characteristics of new Nigerian poetry that, in the opinion of this researcher, has tampered with the sublimity of the craft of poetry. We may surmise that Raji picks on soft images and symbols obviously not only because he has a particular audience target, but also because he, during his sojourn in the US, encountered several other poets on the other side of the Atlantic whose works may have influenced him. The lucidity of diction, the non-acute imagery, and the pliable, ductile, symbolism, along with what Derek Walcott calls the "phenomenal arrogance [of] American syntax" (quoted in Ayewanu 27) in American literature can be infectious. Raji's audience, he says, after all, is the American people. Raji's thinking here is contentious because a writer who has already acquired an audience cannot afford to disappoint his audience for another audience if at all a writer considers his craft subservient to the wishes of an audience.

There are fifteen poems, of various lengths, in *Shuttlesongs America*. They are not compartmentalised into thematic sections as we see in Raji's other collections. Each title is a name of a place visited by the enthusiastic poet-tourist. The poems carry feelings of strangeness, love, hate, humility, surprise and, indeed, a kaleidoscopic inquest into the multi-racial nature of the American society. In these personal-cum-historical poems, we have the untiring poet who undertakes, in his own words, "too deliberate exploration of the persistence of dream, vision and a surprising loneliness" (*Shuttlesongs America* ix). In very bold terms, the poet interrogates racism, not in the anti-racist racist manner of earlier African writers such as Ayi Kwei Armah , engages multi-racialism, in a no less critical manner, and adumbrates the dishonesty and the crisis of existence in a society that, in the loudest (though pretentious) voices, proclaims human justice.

"Kalamazoo" announces the arrival of the poet in a strange land which as he says is better than his own land. "I arrived light" (2) almost carries the tone of someone who is out of a prison, out of captivity, a tone that may have denigrating effect on the country of the poet. This is not surprising since the poet, through his trajectory, has presented himself as a poet who is not just out to be critical of events in his country but to engage the military oppressor in a combat. Given the oppression in his land, coming out of it, landing in the US which, in all intents and purposes, proclaims human freedom, the poet indeed may have "arrived light". But he says his steps are "heavy with the dust of an ancient / civilization" (3-4). Is this Raji's contribution to the Achebean argument that Africa had its civilisation ever before the white people came? The line dispels the earlier tone of anti-nationhood, the poet now asserting his own civilisation, though "ancient", in a land that civilisation, at least within the confines of the poet's innocence, is an overwhelming light. Raji's conclusion here is that the US is a land of civilisation, a land of light, an opinion hinged on what he has seen on arrival, although, as we will see shortly, he will begin to question the civilisation whose presence is so felt here. Raji then introduces himself as a poet to the new land; he is a "singer of dimple songs" (5). His songs, in his own perception, are those of love and life and the endurance one needs to live through hardship. The "unsung tales / of [his] native land..." (6-7) which the poet carries in his chest is metaphoric of the captivity of his tongue or pen as a poet in his own land. The atmosphere in the new land may now make him sing those tales, given the new civilisation-cum-freedom. That is why he seeks "New dreams, new faces, new / souls" (8-9) which will enable him operate properly (indeed, freely) in the new land. The seasonal weather of the new strange land, "Spring in my feet, summer on my brow" (10), which definitely contrasts that of his land, will, in a way, enhance the new poetic inspiration that he is beginning to have. At the end of what we may see as his survey of a land that appears to be favourable to his craft, the poet finally asserts his poetic presence, idiom, tropes and all: "I, name-sake of laughter..."(11). Laughter has been a telling idiom of survival in Raji's corpus, a *manner* of singing the songs of survival in the time of military oppression.

The poet, who has felt his feet on the soil of the US, sings his songs, increasingly, not about the oppression in the land he came from, but about the fascination of the cities in the US. In these diverse songs, the poet is in the process of self-inscription, negation and affirmation, curiously, consciously, trying to avoid, though without success, that sense of hybridity. He tries to see himself not inscribed in the American dream, the American culture, trying hard to assert his *Nigerianness*, especially where it is difficult to assert. Thus, in each description of the cities of the US, he sees himself reflected against the template of the history of struggle and survival. In "Chicago", for instance, the poet celebrates the bustling that goes on in Chicago, a popular city in the US. Chicago is introduced as a city where "possibilities / become realities" (1-2), a very *Nigerian* way of valuing the US. There is a scene of cow milk production that shows another nature of the city of Chicago; it is popular for its bulls, a characteristic it shares with most, if not all, African societies. The poet-tourist takes us to a scene of "plastic juke box houses / of little lives / in the South" (10-2). The picture here is that of the history of the black Americans' suffering, in almost the same manner that Nigerians suffer under the military. They are the "little lives" of the "South." Their history gives the poet an image in which "Dream and Nightmare walk / hand in hand" (15-6). There is a critical tone here as Raji cannot afford to be an uncritical poet in the face of such a history, *another* history. Then he takes us to Michigan's lake, whose surrounding is dirty. He walks all alone here "Past the town-crier of Chi-cow-go's / history" (19-20). Raji's pun on "Chicago" here seems to contemptibly reduce the status of the city probably because of its bitter history. The history seems anti-human since it creates, for the poet, a nightmare and also because it has made the lake ugly when it "can be more beautiful" (30). This is also the story of Africa, of Raji's Nigeria.

In reading "River Kalamazoo", the reader has the sense that the poems in this collection do not only have a common atmosphere, but also have an organic link. There is something inherently American running through the poems, somewhat *alienating* the poems, as strange as it seems, from the poet himself. River Kalamazoo is one of the numerous symbols in the collection that achieve alienation between the poet and his poems, the versification of American cultural matrices. The poet-tourist and his companions are riding canoes on the river. It is on a "Sunday summer noon" (1). Katherine leads the show possibly trying to educate the other on riding on the river. The river, the poet says, may not be "too deep" (9), but "It is long in breath and brown with age" (10). This may be one of the things that make it a tourist attraction. The fun of riding on water certainly has its own problem. The poet shows this when he says, "...the canoe took a dive" (17) and all except the woman leading become afraid. Of course all is not well as "Hrisee and Djoko lost the track / Their canoe surely missed the pack" (26-27). Their fun seems to be short-lived as they "needed a fishing crew / To save the day!" (31-32). The flow of the river is the flow of American essence, a society that offers a *dangerous* pleasure, especially for the poet-tourist whose homeland lacks genuine pleasure. In every of his moves, in every of his keen observations, in all his mental assessment of what he sees, the poet-tourist is in the process of discovery, his memory alert, and his faculties incessantly critiquing a society whose *base* and *superstructure* (in the sense Karl Marx uses the terms) provide a startling level of epiphany for the poet-tourist. Raji is perhaps clearer in "Rock N' Roll, Cleveland" where he likens the American dancing hall, where her native music – rock and roll – is sung and danced, to a church "where the gods of music were carved / in wax" (3-4). Raji calls the singers and dancers pilgrims "in search of Elvis the king" (9), the man who is said to have invented the rock and roll music. The poet-tourist desires to see other kinds of music, but he can only see them "cloned in clothes and blaring tubes", (13). In fact, he cannot find "...priest of pristine / melodies "(14-15) which he may have been used to from his own land. Raji's critical stand against the kind of life lived by the American songsters is seen in these lines:

> In that synagogue of sounds
> the road to fame is paved
> With rum, dope, rage and death. (16-8)

It is a music industry full of alcoholism, drug consumption and fatal anger and envies. The American society, as pleasurable as it is, encouraging the people to catch large life, is also paradoxically a land in which there is freedom of violence especially among the musicians and other artists. Singers consumed by such violence come to have fame attached to their names, such as Tupac.

Now and then, Raji also gives us the pure beauty of the American landscapes. We see the wonder of waterfalls in "Niagara Falls". The poet beholds the wonder for just a night, but he experiences much of the wonder, the "syllables of water above / ancient rocks" (3-4), all through his stay in the US, and in such cases implying the sharp contrast between his homeland and the strange land. In a hyperbolic feat, the poet shows the extent of the speed of water in the Falls. Like other places the poet has visited, Niagara Falls has its "heroic tales" (8) which make it a tourist's attraction. The poet writes of the comfortable atmosphere surrounding the place, it is quiet and tender. In the morning,

> Niagara becomes the valley of creation
> The rainbow rises and falls
> in a glorious curve. (15-17)

Rainbow signifies the time and availability of seasonal water. At Niagara, the rains fall unceasingly. Rains add a natural condition to Niagara Falls. The poet is full of admiration for not only the nature and appearance of Niagara Falls, but also for those who have consciously constructed and nurtured it, giving tourists a delight of a lifetime with it. The poet-tourist takes us to a historical site of one of the biggest phenomena in American religion in "Peter Whitmer's / Hill Cumorah." It was on the Hill Cumorah, in New York, that Joseph Smith, founder of Mormons church (also known as The Church of the Latter Day Saints), received his vision and retrieved the gold plates from which the book of Mormons was translated. The Hill Cumorah is a great sight of wonder. Raji's short poem does not say something of the wonder of the hill nor does it bother on the nature of worship of the Mormons. It rather bears a note of satire on religion. He sees "an American Christ / among murmuring natives" (3-4) in the latter religion. What this suggests immediately is that religion, Christianity, has undergone so much of domestication – and quite radical ones – that self-made Christs abound in it. And the most troubling point about such domestication, which Raji satirises here, is that such religions are, in most cases, religions of mere fashions because "you will not find the answer to so many / Gomorrah questions" (6-7) in them, or they are means used to oppress the poor, the unarmed. Gomorrah is a symbol of sins from the human nature. Raji's inscription of Gomorrah in American process of religious formation here is to, as it were, reiterate the dominant tone of the collection, i.e. satirising the huge irony that is the American society. Religion is worth satirising because it is one of the machineries used in promoting racism and hostility.

"Seneca Falls", one of the engaging poems in the collection, has a socio-feministic history. Seneca Falls, in 1848, housed one of the radical movements of the *freedom ferment* of the early nineteenth century in the U.S organized by Lucretia Mott and Elizabeth Cady Stanton. About two hundred and forty sympathisers, among them forty men, including the famous abolitionist, Frederick Douglas, attended the Seneca Falls Convention. The convention came up with a number of resolutions, modelled on the American declaration of independence, which aimed at women's suffrage, marital reforms and property laws so that women should move out of their inferior status in the society. The poet-tourist confesses his love and admiration for the courage of "the women at Seneca / Falls" (1-2). In doing this he identifies with the women's cause. More than that he perceives the women's cause as epical:

> The ones' who dared, who wrote
> and wrapped their names
> In the sentiment of that glorious
> Declaration. (3-6)

The poet is excited to be on the same ground with those brave women treading the paths they trod, and beholding "their bodies / In that corridor of history" (8-9). The poet becomes more emboldened to drum about the significance and valour of mothers in any society. In the hyperbolic essence of his praise of women, Raji talks of "God the Mother" (12). This poem, having a different theme from Raji's other poems about women, has its distinctive class in his corpus.

"New York" is a fairly long poem that takes its course from the praise of New York City as a large, multi-racial one, to the plight of the Afro-Americans of the Harlem's history. Somehow the poet here is so fascinated by the sites that he does not bite with his usual critical images. New York is the city

Of Greenwich Village and SoHo
Chinatown and Little Italy
Central Park and Harlem... (4-6)

Echoed in the names are some of the races that the poet encounters
in the bustling city. Again, here the poet is critical of the American
society especially in how it has handled multi-racialism. As a
stranger, the poet-tourist walks alone in the throng of these races
seeing people of different origins and this "could really be
beautiful" (9); the enthusiasm is unmistakable. The poet-tourist
watches the orderliness of everyone, "Through the million throng"
(20), going about his business. He picks a literary allusion from
Ralph Ellison's *The Invisible Man*, likening himself – or any
stranger on that land – to Ellison's major character whose society
does not care whether he exists or not. Or, to put it in the racially
constructed circumstances of Ellison's novel, the terrible reality
that a black man, no matter his talents and capability, is an
invisible man in a society that is principally hostile to the kind of
skin he possesses. So, in the throngs of New York, any person is
"just a struggling style / in the memory of steps" (27-28) because
everyone is so busy pursuing his job and no one cares who anyone
is. The society too, as a matter of racism, does not care how the
coloured people fare, the dangers they face, the uncertainties of
their existence. Such people are, of course, the immigrants.
Mention is made of Ellis Island, historically famous for being the
island where immigrants from Europe first set their feet on the
American soil. In Ellis Island, there are pictures and albums of
names of migrants from mostly Eastern Europe and Germany
(mostly Jews fleeing the Nazi regime). Most Europeans living in
America today go there to trace their origins. Raji captures this
situation in these lines:

I have set my feet on Ellis Island
Which took in the original migrants
from dying Europe
Unending figures and facts assailed my sight

And the pilgrimage is endless
For those seeking their pints of blood
In the family album of willing settlers. (29-34)

"Dying Europe" refers to the wars and recession that flushed people from Europe to America. The "pilgrimage" (34) of such people is "endless" (34) because most of them now see Ellis Island as their native land or as the only link to their native lands. For the fact that they carry a wounded history and a remembrance of whatever second-class-citizen treatment they might have received, the poet points out that *"The flies of Ellis bit with a vengeance"* (Italics his, 37). Either vengeance against the native Americans or against their lost native lands. It is also one of the reasons that violence bustle in such a society. The poet then leads us to "the streets / of Harlem West and East" (38-39). Here, we feel the elegiac tone of

...the vanishing souls of a race
Marcus Garvey, Malcom X, Martin
Luther King, Bobby Seale and
the terrible tigers
Richard Wright, Claude Mckay
and Langston Hughes the Muse. (41-6)

Harlem has lost most of these great writers and freedom fighters. They all have one cause or the other to rise against the oppression of the American racism. Again, like we see in "Seneca Falls" Raji identifies with them readily. At one level, what these heroes have passed through is what he and others are currently passing through in his native land, Nigeria. The vision is shared. Gradually, the poet-tourist is discovering himself among the names and the people he sees here. At another level, the poet-tourist feels intellectually awakened in Harlem. This is even more important because, Raji, as a researcher of Afro-American Literature and Culture, has taught most (if not all) of these great thinkers and he is thus equipped to know and feel them on this native soil of theirs:

> I walked where they once spoke
> I walked where they once walked
> Their footprints faintly seen
> under the plasters of new terraces. (47-50)

We see here that modernity has crept into the native land of the Afro-American people as the last line above shows. The poet is worried about this modernisation, which of course may erode the concrete symbols of a painful history, and asks:

> Harlem, where are your cafes
> Which spawned a regime of writers and
> dancers, where are your myths? (51-53)

This question is vital because it signposts the fact that the American authority may not have done enough to preserve a history that should be there to perpetually remind the white American people of a time that man was indeed inhuman to his fellow man. The answer to the poet's question is that as he, as well as everyone, can see, Harlem's myths are already confined to museums and the tenement houses of Harlem "give way now / To glittering stores / Which maul the pocket" (57-9). The American modernity has done something to the original face of Harlem. Raji's tone is that of disappointment.

The poet however likes what he sees of Philadelphia as recounted in "Philadelphia." It is a home peopled by men and women of his nature and that is why he moves about in it "like a veteran" (3). Even the weather, i.e. the sunshine of Philadelphia is African-like. This makes the poet enjoys the tour, entering church, market and other popular and highly populated streets. The ironic twist to this is that the poet nurses hatred for Philadelphia after all because he fears her "police record" (46) against his "color" (47) because Philadelphia carries a history of racism in her armpit despite her beautiful, weather-friendly appearance. Raji continues his theme of slavery and racism in "Williamsburg" and "Jamestown." The former – with its name symbolic of the human waste in Virginia area in those days –

contains two standing symbols that are important to the history of America: "the open museum" (1) and the re-enactment of the war scene of "November 17, 1775" (7). The poet-tourist, although fascinated by the artistic re-enactment of the slavery business of the old days, is awed by the immensity of man's inhumanity to man. What he sees also reminds him of the American war to gain her independence from the British Empire. It is in Willamsburg that the poet-tourist actually encounters the past of wasted humanity that might have given rise to the hope of today and tomorrow:

Williamsburg bubbled
in the remembrance
of things done, undone and re-done
Williamsburg is the past
which reshapes a people's future. (18-22)

The place called Colonial Williamsburg, in Virginia, is a place set aside to remind people of the past and the poet-tourist's feeling here shows that it does so quite well. In "Jamestown", Raji subtly attacks the actors of slave trade, responsible for shipping slaves from Africa to America. In a manner point blank, he says "Jamestown, there's a gap in the teeth / of your history" (1-2). The gap is created by the inhumanity of slave trade. He mentions the historical reality that a ship sailed for 144 days, missing, before it found its way to Jamestown. After seeing all the remains of the slavery and "John Povy's brilliant blasphemy" (22), the poet asks, with a painful concern for the Africans enslaved:

Tell me, who worked the maize
and tobacco farms
for the Virginia Company of London?
Beasts or men, names or numbers
Who made the quilt that robed the land?
Who planted the profits of gold
by crude labor? (26-32)

These questions, rhetorical as they are, attempt to plumb the cruel hearts that set humanity on the course of slave trade, the worst human condition since the creation of man. They also bring to the fore the greed and aggrandisement the white people had at the back of their minds when they set out to capture the black people into slavery. Raji is, here, treading the paths of radical historians and writers who have accused the Europeans and Americans of impoverishing the African continent right from the beginning of days.

The poet-tourist lands us in Washington D.C., the capital city of the US. His explorations are still centred on the monumental and historic sites of the great country. He is fascinated by Romanesque parks and by the Library of Congress in Washington D.C. He comes in contact with the wonder of the Smithsonian Museum in the city:

> ...Myths and designs and lore
> locked in Smithson's house of legends.
> *Natural History, Arts and Industry*
> *Air & Space, Hirshhorn, ...African Art.* (italics his, 10-13)

The art works collected in this museum are not those of America alone, but they are collected from all parts of the world. Raji uses "Nogbaisi and his family of bronze / carvings" (15-16) to represent the Nigerian art works taken to Europe and America. They are abandoned in the museum, according to the poet-tourist, because they are sitting uselessly in halls. In the kingdom in which these bronze carvings were produced, they would have been more functional, spiritually meaningful than in the US where they are just kept to be only watched for tourist purposes. They are symbols of Western enslavement of the African continent, which, in spite of persistent cries of restitution, have remained in the West just to remind and amuse them of the suppression and oppression they had subjected Africans to. Being the last city, and the most important city of the US, the poet is traversing, he focuses on the inhumanity of slavery in a reassessment of a society that is so warm and yet is built on contours of hostility. In the museum are images of American *forced* multi-racialism and multi-culturality.

Like the race of the poet, every other race, such as the Asian, the Caribbean, the Arab, will see a history of violence against their race reflected on the shelves and on the wall of the Smithsonian Museum. Obviously, the poet Raji is overwhelmed by what he has seen, i.e. the dual existence, and the seemingly seam blending of the diversity, of humanism and anti-humanism in the same cultural setting. The American preservation of memories, then, has a way of giving one a sense of anger, seeing his race and history, as well as giving one a sense of inspiration towards understanding the multi-cultural matrix of the American society. Kalamazoo, now symbol of the beginning and source of poetic power as well as inspirational tour-guide, is invoked by the poet here:

> Kalamazoo of gentle night
> Forgive me if I forget a paddle in the
> boat
> My memory is long, my breath is
> Short. (Italics his, 27-31)

The "boat" here is symbolic of the tour. The poet does not claim to have a total control of his memory but he has acquired a lot in the cavity of his memory.

In this poetic travelogue, maybe the first of its kind in Nigerian poetry, the poet-tourist does not only tour, but also makes serious commentaries on the issues of man's inhumanity to man such as slavery and racism. The American society, both past and present, as portrayed in Raji's poetic sensibility, is an enslaver. Raji is from one of the races that are victims of American and European enslavement of the black people. In his admiration and eulogy of the great monuments and edifices in America, there is a subtle criticism of the American society especially in the way it treats African-Americans, embeds the jewellery of the African race in her history for purposes of amusement and tourism. The poet-tourist begs to *return tenderly* (37) to his land because he knows that despite the pleasure the American structure offers now, the poet can only feel comfortable in his own land. The American society, in a sense, is a place where a black man is confronted with his history which may haunt him all his life.

The remaining two poems in this collection are "Flakes" and "Flares", written for separate occasions while the poet was still in the US, but having less or nothing of the enthusiasm of the poet-tourist, and being less critical of the American philosophy. "Flakes" captures an unpleasant situation that the poet went through while delayed at JF Kennedy Airport in New York. To the poet, the world seems to have turned upside down. Hence he arranges the numbers, written in roman numerals, from X to I, in a descending order, instead of from I to X. Storm may have been responsible for the airport delay because the poem opens with the description of the weather, so strange to the poet's "tropical feet" (5):

> Sandstorms...
> Windstorm...
> Snowstorm... (1-3)

These are weather realities in Europe and the US that are capable of holding activities to a standstill. The weather is so chilly that the poet experiences what he refers to as "mocking coldness" (8). At such times, the sun becomes "cosmetic" (10) since the winter overpowers it. In the next stanza, the poet describes snowstorm thus:

> The flaky white dust
> The battering male wind
> The skin-deep strings
> Icicles of rain without water
> Embodied and whitened storms
> This is my first story of snow... (11-16)

Coming from the tropical part of the world, this experience is bound to be strange to the poet. The poet's feeling here is definitely a mixed one because he is fascinated by this new experience and he knows that he is marooned at the airport because of this condition. He falls an easy prey to the gripping cold which makes

him go "Numb to the world" (17-18). He has to put on some
cardigans on top of each other to survive the biting cold. He says:
"I become the onion of a thousand cloths" (20). It is by doing so
that he can survive. He describes the weather again, saying "...the
sky" (22) appears like "the saw-millers pastime" (23). His thought
is not far away from him; it is on the surrounding pine trees,
now coated in snow-dust, which he can see. Two voices, obviously
those of the white people, sympathise with him because of his
reaction to the snowstorm. The poet tells them (and there is a
tone of superiority here) that "Unfortunately, my nation knows
no / flakes / no tornadoes, no earthquakes..." (33-35). What
this implies is that because the poet's land has none of those things,
it is indeed a better land. The poet casts his philosophic mind on
the strange land. It is the seeking of knowledge that has brought
him to the land "Where Nature nullifies all knowledge / And
Science becomes trapped in her / own laboratory of incest" (39-
41). Something paradoxical and satirical is discerned here. Despite
man's knowledge and achievement in science and technology,
nature – the weather – cannot be tamed in man's knowledge
and exploits. God owns nature and man owns science. That
nature is greater than science is, no doubt, natural. The poet
mentions his fellow country people whose "Voices give [him] the
pleasure of / robes" (42-3). They may have given him
encouragement and words of advice through the phone while he
is that helpless at the airport. They are Akin, Olakunle, Pius, Wumi
and Unoma. They are all Nigerians, probably resident in the US
and are not, unlike the poet, new to the weather. The poet will
definitely leave for his land. But he also knows that to this strange
land he will return. This means this is just his first trip to the US
and cannot be the last, no matter the experience now. It is the
"compulsion to know" (60), that intellectual inquest, that will
bring him back. Raji's attitude to the American snowstorms is
that of dismay especially as it balks him from going his way, and
this is strange to a man, from Africa, where such horrendous
weather does not exist. Raji is proud of his land in his comparison

of the American weather to that of his country. But the essence of man as a slave to knowledge (as we see in Alfred Lord Tennyson's "Ulysses") will put the poet on his way to this land again, despite the inclement weather.

The last part of this collection is titled "Flare" – a sequence of poems in which the poet-tourist takes to deep, philosophical thoughts on his life in a strange land and the strangeness of the land seen in the many sites and images he traverses and allows his imagination to work on. The lines here are specifically produced to mark his birthday that came while he was still in the US. The poems were done in November 2001 while the poet was a visiting scholar at Southern Illinois University, Edwardsville. Raji, in his author's note, points out that "This was a moment I would be consciously aware of an approaching birthday and that in a 'foreign' land" (viii). In these poetic meditations, Raji takes a discursive course, touching a number of issues that primarily affect his life, reminding him of where he hails from, creating in him a stranger's awareness, giving him the insight to study the people and places he now lives in and equipping him with a renewed philosophy with which to live on in a world full of noonday mystery. Raji plays with the number 1, 9, 6, and 1 as numbers of the titles, although they are actually the numbers that come together to form the year of his birth, 1961. Thus we have "#1: Opening page", a short poem in which the poet refers to himself as "the book of memory, unread, / unknown..." (7-8). Contained in this book are "the secret of multiple / thoughts" (3-4). The thoughts carry tenderness for humanity. We are already acquainted with the Rajian laughter that claims to bring succour to humanity. This is what the poet refers to here. In the second poem "#9: If this poem could only speak", the poet talks of a time when words become impotent and the mouth loses its speech; "Such time when words lay waste / splayed, insensate" (1-2). But the impotence of the words may also have been occasioned by the fact that "violence makes a home / in the teeth of words" (7-8). Words can be used by a man to inflict pain on another man. It can also be that words are dead because "the tongues is torn / In an orphanage of spite / and despair" (12-14). When words do not bear any importance again, as has been pointed out, the poet says, "It's all wise to speak with the eye" (17). It appears that Raji attempts to *thingify* the severe effect of loneliness on his speech or pen capacity. For in a strange land, among strange people, looking is surely wiser than speaking. Looking then has temporarily rendered the poet inactive.

"#6: One with mystery" has a dense texture with tough images. The poet seems to have found comfort in his loneliness. He begins by saying "A loneliness all too lovely with mindful / tidings" (1-2). He goes on to describe the kind of society he has found himself in. He is faced with "robed greetings" (4) and busy days. This loneliness creates "prisons of the mind" (8) for him. In this prison, things become mystical. The poet at once acquires "the gift of precision, of vision, / and of predictions" (9-10). He fathoms the mystery of the wind, coming to understand the deep inside of the wind. Here, the poet-persona begins to understand hallucination in a strange land. He even levitates and it is at this realm that "everything is mystery" (19) to him. Those things that have turned mystical to him include:

    the first finger of Light
    the tame tongue of the sun
    the rustling silence through the footpath
    the hysteria of birds and squirrels
    the snake's evening greeting
    the deer's wink like a lady's fast smile
    the cruel precision of the postmaster
    the incredible fiction of freedom where
    everywhere you turn to is an open prison. (20-28)

The poet's summation here is that things in his life that are ordinarily normal have turned mystical with the loneliness he finds himself in. Yet we see the distortion of natural things in what confronts him as daily activities. Already he says earlier that the wind is "technicolor" (14). The tongue of the sun is tamed.

The next lines take us to a place like a wildlife park. We are shown a place redolent of the African forest as we see the daily running of the birds, the squirrels, the snakes and the deer. All of these, in a land of loneliness, in a land of "incredible fiction of freedom", in a land of "open prison", make life a mystery where the poet is even afraid of the possibilities that abound in his own mind. At such a time, nature holds out its warmth and hospitality. Hence the poet says:

> I speak with the stars
> I moan with the wind
> In love with my heart's lake
> An inner warmth, yet lonely and cold. (34-37)

The poet-persona is not comfortable with this condition even though he talks, at the beginning, of loneliness with mindful tidings. But it is not loneliness that frustrates him. His struggle with the strangeness of the foreign land makes him one with mystery.

The next sequence, "#1: Whisper", looks at the inward power of loneliness that shows through the cathartic consequences of solitude. The poet-persona has come to know, ultimately, of the strength that resides in the inside of a lonely man. It is clear that "the journey must begin / with a will to swim / towards that light within" (4-6). A person must first heal himself from the inside, i.e. purify himself from within. And when that is done, "The world will go mad, and [he] will not" (9-10). For this, the poet-persona points out that solitude will always win at the end of it all. Raji returns to the images of animals, as we find in *A Harvest*, in "#9: Transformation." The poet-persona sees himself as a sunbird (owner of the sky), as an earthworm (owner of the earth) and as a starfish (owner of the water). He is thus ubiquitous in a sense. More than that, he now possesses a tripartite medium of looking at the world in order to get a wider, deeper and more philosophical picture of the world. Really, he is a more mature person. While a sunbird, he is high above, but paradoxically sees "the smallest thought / of the slimmest woman" (4-5). He even sees the skeletons of worms and, in a more incisive metaphor, sees and suspects "the kidneys of men as / hidden bombs" (8-9). In every atom of the American society, there is something that is noxious to humanity. A heavy metaphor with a philosophical import comes in the next line: "In every heart, there's a grinding / stone" (10-11). What this suggests is that every heart has a place for grinding (considering) a thought or an idea before letting it out. Man is made to think. Whatever a man lets out of himself will be good or bad depending on how he has used his grinding stone. It also suggests that all actions, especially the actions he encounters in the strange land, are deliberate. Then the poet-persona becomes an earthworm. He feels "the nitrogen of hate buried in the / skin of all" (13-14). He is concerned with the attitude of men to their fellow men because he also sees "mounds of / malice" (15-6) and in his search for love he only sees "the peroxide of pain" (22). So all around him, as an earthworm, he cannot find love and brotherhood the type characteristic of Africa. Then he becomes a starfish. He is "In search of the watery mystery of / survival" (25-26). He has to survive in the midst of sharks, and to do that, he has to "perch on the wings" of his soul (29). Raji uses the images of animals to present survival in a strange land. Even when he transforms, the poet-persona only moves from one stage of existence to the other, still with the need to survive. Hence survival is a continuous thing. And it can be made easy if the person in the game of survival understands that each heart has a grinding stone and uses it effectively.

The last poem in the sequence, "#1: Abiku", presents Raji not just as a poet-persona musing over a lonely birthday with an adjustable spirit, but also as a poet with a flexible craft. Already, it has been mentioned how Raji internationalises his poetry by descending from the dense imagery of the African poetry to the soft, prosaic imagery of American poetry. In this poem, Raji seems to be saying that he has the Abiku spirit and people should not be surprised of his changes in nature. Raji dwells on the physical appearance of the Abiku child who is normally disfigured with cuts and incisions and comes back with the same marks. But beyond this picture of Abiku, Raji's hidden meaning is that although he finds himself in America and most of the things Americans do, such as even the style of their poetry become infectious to him, he still knows quite well that he is rooted in his homeland, in his culture and tradition.

One of Raji's consistent thematic points throughout the poems in this collection is that he is proud of his African origin and soil and he has, more than this, taken a mild swipe at the colonial masters as well as drummed up praises for Africans (and non-Africans) who were actors of revolt against slavery. This is at the core of Raji's nationalist imagination at the transnational level. Raji fully realises himself as a poet, an African poet, aware of his African realities in a land so different from Africa.

# CHAPTER
# 8

## Conclusion

The purpose of this research work has been to locate and canonise Remi Raji's poetry within the mainstream of literature of social commitment in Nigeria. A dominant tradition of the socially committed art is the writer's utmost desire to commit his writing to the welfare of the state. In doing so, he positions his art between the people and the establishment, rising against the latter on behalf of the former. This tradition has continued to exist in Nigerian literature since its beginning. The tradition becomes even more dominant in Raji's era given the fact that writers of this period, mostly born in the 1960s, have been the most unfortunate to witness the evils of military dictators and their civilian collaborators in Nigeria. In fact, most of them, as we have pointed out earlier, are victims of the state of anomie that gripped Nigeria in the 1980s and 1990s. The political theme of this period, as we have demonstrated with Raji's poetry, often captures the years of despondency occasioned by the almost thirty years of military rule in Nigeria, and the failure of politicians to rescue the nation when they took over from the military.

Having produced five volumes of poetry, with a vision conscious of nationhood, Raji has become a stable, dependable and enduring voice in recent Nigerian poetry. A poet with a consummate political theme, Raji sees versification as an engagement in the socio-political discourse of his land, aimed at forging a just nation. He believes that a poet should pursue "the possibilities of connecting poetry and pure nationalism" (*Sou'wester*, 10). He sees himself as a singer for the masses, vigorously set to "remember and make others remember the havoc of yesterday's flood, the twitches in the twilight of lives, the madness in moonlit intrigues and the blindness in the illumination of day" (*Webs*, 9). Raji's mettle as a poet is more noticeable in his political poems through which he combats the oppressor and gives succour to the oppressed, and the interpretation of these poems is the concern of this book. Raji's corpus till date consists of *A Harvest of Laughters* (1997), *Webs of Remembrance* (2001), *Shuttlesongs: America – A Poetic Guided Tour* (2003), *Lovesong for My Wasteland* (2005), and *Gather My Blood Rivers of Song* (2009). He develops his imagery with significant ardour and maturity. The first thing that will interest a reader of Raji' poetry is the eloquence Raji brings into harnessing words to create sharp and incisive images either in attacking the bad leaders or in sympathising with those who are oppressed. The poet is both concerned with the plight of the ordinary citizenry and the writers/journalists, that species of the society's elite who cannot keep silent in the face of oppression.

Raji's aesthetics of resistance – and, indeed, that of other poets writing in Nigeria today – can effectively be understood through the sociological approach. To begin with, the poet himself stands out as a person whose consciousness has been widened to the extent that he no longer wants to stomach the incurable ineptitude of the military despotism and leadership failure. Out of this consciousness and an abiding zeal to fight the status quo, the poet sings his songs, as it were, which are full of criticism and satire against the oppressor. The poet's intention is to let his audience know of the evils that are responsible for the country's stagnation and, thereafter, to incite the people against the oppressor. To those who cannot fight, who have lost any hope of survival, the poet gives hope through tender images that point to a fruitful future. For Raji, "the journey is certainly from the darkness to light" (*Sou'wester*, 12).

We have also tried to delineate the effect of historical facts on Raji's poetry and vice versa. Raji's large claim is that he writes poetry for the sake of his nation. This is why his poetry bears, as well as constructs, a large chunk of Nigerian history of subjugation through protracted military dictatorship and, now, a rapacious civilian government. Raji's political poetry attempts to historicise this moral and political collapse in Nigeria and my contention here is that he has done it so appreciably well that his poetry has come to deserve this critical attention.

We have pointed out that Raji begins his enterprise by defining himself and understanding the vision before him. To this extent, he sees himself as the bearer of the therapeutic laughter that has come to become a vital metaphor in the summation of his poetic vision. Laughter is a metaphorical weapon not only for the poet but also for those who suffer along with him, with which they can endure the socio-political condition of their society. His social vision is to see himself and his people, the common people, endure with the kind of laughter that disarms the oppressors' stings. We therefore dwell a great deal on Raji's trope of laughter which he uses as a handle for ploughing from pessimism to optimism through the rough terrain of bad governance in his society. Raji's poetic attack on the past military leaders, as seen in *A Harvest, Webs of Remembrance* and on the moneyed, totalitarian civilian government, as seen in *Gather My Blood*, cuts him out as perhaps the openly bitterest poet writing in Nigeria today. In his first two volumes, Raji's tone is, first, that of anger as well as combat, and, second, that of a belief in a future that will certainly come at the end of the bleak period. In *Lovesong*, Raji comes out more invigorated to pull his society out of its stagnancy with stronger poetry of optimism. The thematic thrust is that the havoc of yesterday perpetrated by the leaders who are inept and mindless in their governance does not – and should not – bring down the nation into the kind of collapse that will stagnate it forever. In this volume of choreo-poetry, Raji presents a prescience of transcendence. In *Gather My Blood*, Raji interrogate the post-military democracy that fails to give the Nigerian citizenry a just society. In *Shuttlesong America*, Raji, in another sphere of social criticism, looks beyond Nigeria, interrogates racism and the huge paradox that is the United States of America.

This work presents Raji in totality as a political poet. Running themes and motifs in his poetry show that he is a poet consistent with his vision of seeing the suffering ones in his society given succour, and of seeing the land ultimately liberated from wolves who parade themselves as leaders. A basic point of conclusion is that Raji is a poet who cannot be ignored in our canon of contemporary Nigerian poetry. In fact, he stands out prominent as a political poet because of his developed poetics, his social vision and considerable output. This study has tried to bring this out as a contribution to the ongoing discourse on committed writing in Nigerian, African and world literatures.

# Works Cited

## Primary Sources

Raji, Remi. *Gather My Blood Rivers of Song*. Ibadan: Diktaris, 2009

_____. *Lovesong for my Wasteland*. Ibadan: Bookcraft, 2005.

_____. *Shuttlesongs: America – A Poetic Guided Tour*. Ibadan: Bookcraft, 2003.

_____. *Webs of Remembrance*. Ibadan: Kraftgriots, 2001.

_____. *A Harvest of Laughters*. Ibadan: Kraftgriots, 1997.


## Secondary Sources

Abdu, Saleh. *Poet of the People's Republic: Reading the Poetry of Niyi Osundare*. Kano: Benchmarks, 2003.

Achebe, Chinua. *The Trouble with Nigeria*. Enugu: Fourth Dimension, 1984.

_____. *Morning Yet on Creation Day: Essays*. London: Heinemann, 1977.

Adeniyi, Olusegun. *The Last 100 Days of Abacha: Political Drama in Nigeria Under One of Africa's Most Corrupt and Brutal Military Dictatorships*. Lagos: Bookhouse, 2005.

Adepitan, Titi. "Issues in Recent African Writing." *African Literature Today*. 25. (2006): 124-8.

Adewale, Toyin. Introduction. *25 New Nigerian Poets*. Berkeley:

Ishmael Reed Publishing, 2000.

Adichie, Chimamanda N. *Purple Hibiscus*. Lagos: Farafina, 2004.

Aiyejina, Funso. "Recent Nigerian Poetry in English: An Alter-Native Tradition." *Perspectives on Nigerian Literature: 1700 to the Present*. Ed. Yemi Ogunbiyi. Lagos: Guardian Books, 1988. 112-1280.

Ajibade, Kunle. *Jailed for Life: A Reporter's Prison Notes*. Ibadan: Heinemann, 2003.

Akpuda, Austine Amanze. *Celebrating God's Own Robot: Nigerian Poets and the Gani Fahewinmi Phenomenon*. Owerri: Whytem Publishers, 2003.

Amuta, Chid. "Literature of the Nigerian Civil War." *Perspectives on Nigerian Literature: 1700 to the Present*. Ed. Yemi Ogunbiyi. Lagos: Guardian Books, 1988. 85-92.

Armah, Ayi Kwei. *The Eloquence of the Scribes: A Memoir on the Sources and Resources of African Literature*. Popenguine: Per Ankh, 2006.

_____. *The Beautytiful Ones Are Not Yet Born*. London: Heinemann, 1975.

Atta, Sefi. *Everything Good Will Come*. Lagos: Farafina, 2005.

Anyidoho, Kofi. "Prison as Exile/Exile as Prison: Circumstances, Metaphor, and a Paradox of Modern African Literature." *The Word Behind the Bars and the Paradox of Exile*. Ed. Kofi Anyidoho. Illinois: Northwestern UP 1997. 1-17.

Azuah, Unoma. Interview with Nnorom Azuonye. *Sentinel Poetry Quarterly*. 4. April, 2005. 24-35.

Bakhtin, Mikhail B. *Rabelais and His World*. Trans. Helene Iswolsky. Bloomington and Indianapolis: Indiana University Press, 1984.

Beier, Ulli. "Rabearivelo." Ed. Ulli Beier. *Introduction to African Literature: an Anthology of Critical Writing from 'Black Orpheus'.* London: Longman, 1967. 89-94.

Bly, Robert. *Talking All Morning.* Ann Arbor, Michigan: Michigan UP, 1980. 100-101.

Brown, Stewart. "Still Daring the Beast: Niyi Osundare and Contemporary Nigerian Poetry." *The People's Poet: Emerging Perspectives on Niyi Osundare.* Ed. Abdul-Rasheed Na'Allah. Trenton, NJ: Africa World Press, 2003. 97-113.

Dasylva, Ademola O. and Jegede B. Oluwatoyin. *Studies in Poetry.* Ibadan: Stirling-Horden Publishers, 2005.

Chinweizu, et al. *Towards the Decolonization of African Literature: African Fiction and Poetry and their Critics.* Enugu: Fourth Dimension, 1980.

Caroll, David. "The Post-Literary Condition: Sartre, Camus and the Question(s) of Literature." *The Question of Literature: the Place of the Literary in Contemporary Theory.* Ed. Elizabeth Beaumont Bissell. Manchester: Manchester UP, 2002. 67-90.

Darthone, O. R . "A Study of Two Poems: Christopher Okigbo Understood." *African Literature Today.* 1-4. (1972):

Eagleton, Terry. *Literary Theory: An Introduction.* London: Basil Blackwell Publisher, 1983.

_____. *Criticism and Ideology: A Study in Marxist Literary Theory.* London: Verso Editions, 1978.

Egudu, Romanus N. *The Study of Poetry.* Ibadan: University Press, 1979.

_____. *Modern African Poetry and the African Predicament.* London: Macmillan, 1978

Egya, Sule E. *In Their Voices and Visions: Conversations with New Nigerian Writers.* Lagos: Apex Books, 2007.

_____. "The Nationalist Imagination in Remi Raji's *Lovesong for My Wasteland.*" *Research in African Literatures,* 2007. 38. 4. (2007). 111-126.

_____. "A Critique of the Images of Oppressor in Remi Raji's Poetry." *Ibadan: Journal of English Studies.* 2. (2005): 65-75.

Emezue, Gloria Monica T. *Comparative Studies in African Dirge Poetry.* Enugu: Handel, 2001.

Ezenwa-Ohaeto. *Winging Words: Interviews with Nigerian Writers and Critics.* Ibadan: Kraftbooks, 2003.

_____. *Contemporary Nigerian Poetry and the Poetics of Orality.* Bayreuth: Bayreuth UP, 1998.

Fioupou, Christiane. "The Rope of a Single Idiom: Translating African Poetry." *The People's Poet: Emerging Perspectives on Niyi Osundare.* Ed. Abdul-Rasheed Na'Allah. Trenton, NJ: Africa World Press, 2003. 179-195.

Gates, Henry Louis. "The Blackness of Blackness: A Critique of the Sign and the Signifying Monkey." *Black Literature and Literary Theory.* Ed: Henry Louis Gates Jr. New York: Menthuen, 1984. 285-

Godwin, Ken. *Understanding African Poetry.* London: Heinemann, 1982.

Habila, Helon. *Waiting for an Angel.* London: Penguin, 2002.

Ifowodo, Ogaga. *Homeland and Other Poems.* Ibadan: Kraftgriots, 1998.

Irele, Abiola. "Aime Cesaire: An Approach to His Poetry." *Introduction to African Literature.* Ed. Ulli Beier. London: Longman, 1967. 59-68.

Izevbaye, Dan S. "The State of Criticism in African Literature." *African Literature Today.* Ed. Eldred Durosimi Jones. 7. London:

Heinemann, 1979. 1-19.

Maier, Karl. *This House Has Fallen: Nigeria in Crisis.* London: Penguin, 2000.

Mapanje, Jack. "Containing Cockroaches." Ed. Kofi Anyidoho. *The Word Behind the Bars and the Paradox of Exile.* Illinois: Northwestern UP, 1997. 46-79.

Ndibe, Okey. *Arrows of Rain.* Portsmouth: Heinemann, 2000.

Nduka, Uche. *If Only the Night.* Amsterdam: Sojourner Press, 2002.

_____. (1989) "Ideology, Individual, Poetry: Observations." *Daily Times.* October 18, P. 10.

Njogu, Kimani. *Reading Poetry as Dialogue: An East African Literary Tradition.* Nairobi: JKF, 2004.

Nnolim, Charles E. "African Literature in the 21st Century: Challenges for Writers and Critics." *African Literature Today.* Ed. Ernest N. Emenyonu. 25. Ibadan: Heinemann, 2006. 1-10.

_____. Interview with Austin Amanze Akpuda. *Reconstructing the Canon: Festschrift in Honour of Professor Charles E. Nnolim.* Ed. Austin Amanze Akpuda. Owerri: Treasure Books, 2001. 39-89.

Nwankwo, Agwuncha Arthur. "The Writer and the Politics of His Environment."

*Harvest Time: A Literary/Critical Anthology of the Association of Nigerian Authors Enugu Branch.* Ed. Onuora Ossie Enekwe. Enugu: Snaap Press, 2001. 27-33.

Ofeimun, Odia. "Truth and the Language of Poetry". *Prisms.* 1.1. (2001). 20-24.

Ofeimun, Odia. *The Poet Lied.* Lagos: Update, 1989.

Ojaide, Tanure. Interview with Ezenwa-Ohaeto. *Winging Words: Interviews with Nigerian Writers and Critics*. Ibadan: Kraft Books, 2003. 93-100.

_____. *Poetic Imagination in Black Africa: Essays on African Poetry*. North Carolina: Carolina Academic Press, 1996.

_____. *The Poetry of Wole Soyinka*. Lagos: Malthouse, 1994.

Okara, Gabriel. *The Dreamer, His Vision*. Port Harcourt: UP of Port Harcourt, 2004.

Okigbo, Christopher. *Labyrinths*. Ibadan: Heinemann, 1971.

Okolo, M. S. C. *African Literature as Political Philosophy*. New York: Zed Books, 2007.

Osundare, Niyi. "Soyinka and the Generation After." *Nigerian Newsday Weekly*. 8 Apr. 2005: 21.

_____. Interview with Omowunmi Segun. ALA Bulletin. 25. 4. (Fall 1999): 36-39.

_____. *Songs of the Season*. Ibadan: Heinemann, 1990.

_____. *Songs of Marketplace*. Ibadan: New Horn Press, 1983.

_____. *Waiting Laughters*. Lagos: Malthouse, 1990.

Philip, Nourbese. "Earth and Sound: The Place of Poetry." *The Word Behind the Bars and the Paradox of Exile*. Ed. Kofi Anyidoho. Illinois: Northwestern UP, 1997. 169-182.

Raji, Remi. Interview with Shegun Ajayi. Vanguard Newspaper Online. Internet. August 23 2007.

_____. Interview with Chuks Ohai. *Daily Independent* 15 Sept. 2005: E8.

_____. "Writing Poetry in Praise of the Endangered: The Aesthetics of Rage". Public Lecture given at University of California at Irvine, October, 2003.

_____. Interview with Julie Dill and Matthew Schmitz. *Sou'wester*. (Fall/ Winter, 2001): 9-15.

Reeves, James. *Understanding Poetry*. London: Heinemann, 1965.

Roberts, Phil. *How Poetry Works*. London: Penguin, 2000.

Rotimi, Ola. "Conditions in the Third World: A Playwright's Soliloquy on His Experiences." Ed. Kofi Anyidoho. *The Word Behind the Bars and the Paradox of Exile*. Illinois: Northwestern UP, 1997. 125-133.

Sallah, Tijjan. *New Poets of West Africa*. Lagos: Malthouse, 1995.

Sartre, Jean-Paul. *What is Literature? And Other Essays*. trans: Bernard Frechtman *et. al.* Cambridge, Mass.: Harvard UP, 1948.

Shehu, Emman Usman. *Open Sesame*. Ibadan: Bookcraft, 2005.

Soyinka, Wole. *The Man Died: Prison Notes*. Ibadan: Spectrum, 1985.

Udoeyop, Nyong J. *Three Nigerian Poets: A Critical Study of the Poetry of Soyinka, Clark and Okigbo*. Ibadan: Ibadan UP, 1973.

# Index

Printed in the United States
By Bookmasters